CW00556237

A History of the
Newcastle & Berwick Railway

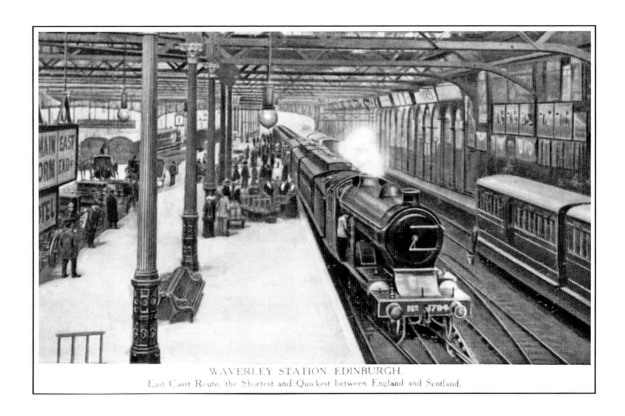

WAVERLEY STATION, EDINBURGH.
East Coast Route, the Shortest and Quickest between England and Scotland.

John F Addyman, Christopher Dean,
Bill Fawcett and Neil Mackay

NORTH EASTERN RAILWAY ASSOCIATION

Copyright © John F Addyman, Christopher Dean, Bill Fawcett and Neil Mackay.

All rights reserved.

No part of this publication may be reproduced, stored in a retrieval system or transmitted, in any form
or by any means, electronic, mechanical, photocopying, recording or otherwise
without prior written permission of the publisher.

Published by the North Eastern Railway Association, January 2011.

ISBN 978 1 873513 75 0

Typeset by John G Teasdale.

Printed in Great Britain by The Amadeus Press.

THE NORTH EASTERN RAILWAY ASSOCIATION

Formed in 1961, the NERA caters for all interested in the railways of north-east England, in particular the North
Eastern Railway and the Hull & Barnsley Railway, from their early history down to the present day. This also extends
to the many industrial and smaller railways that operated alongside them. Interests range over all aspects of
development, operation and infrastructure of the railway, including such diverse activities as locomotive history,
rolling stock, train services, architecture, signalling, shipping, road vehicles and staff matters – both for the general
enthusiast and model maker.

With in excess of 700 members, regular meetings are held in York, Darlington, Hull, and London. A programme
of outdoor visits, tours and walks is also arranged. There is also an extensive library of books, documents,
photographs and drawings available for study by members and non-members alike.

Members receive a quarterly illustrated journal, the NORTH EASTERN EXPRESS, and a newsletter, covering
membership topics, forthcoming meetings and events in the region together with book reviews and a bibliography
of recent articles of interest. Over 200 issues of the EXPRESS have been published to date.

The Association also markets an extensive range of facsimiles of railway company documents, including diagram
books, timetables and other booklets, while at the same time it is developing an expanding range of original
publications, available to members at discounted prices.

For a membership prospectus, please contact:
     K Richardson, Esq, 7 Grenadier Drive, NORTHALLERTON, DL6 1SB. e-mail : membership@ner.org.uk

A list of NERA publications is available. Please send a Stamped Addressed 9" x 4" Envelope to:
     DJ Williamson, Esq, 31 Moreton Avenue, Stretford, MANCHESTER, M32 8BP.

NERA Website : www.ner.org.uk

Contents

Abbreviations used in the text:

A&C : Alnwick & Cornhill Branch
B&T : Blyth & Tyne Railway
BJR : Brandling Junction Railway
BOT : Board of Trade
BR : British Railways
C&HR : Chester & Holyhead Railway
DJR : Durham Junction Railway
ECML : East Coast Main Line
GNBR : Great North British Railway
GNR : Great Northern Railway
LNER : London & North Eastern Railway
LMS : London, Midland & Scottish Railway

N&B : Newcastle & Berwick Railway
N&CR : Newcastle & Carlisle Railway
N&NS : Newcastle & North Shields Railway
NBR : North British Railway
NCR : Northumberland Central Railway
NEIMME : North of England Institute of Mining and Mechanical Engineers
NER : North Eastern Railway
NERA : North Eastern Railway Association
NUR : Northern Union Railway
NYMR : North Yorkshire Moors Railway
OS : Ordnance Survey
WCML : West Coast Main Line
YN&B : York, Newcastle & Berwick Railway

Front cover caption. *The Tweed bridges, completed between 1624 and 1928, viewed from the Newcastle & Berwick Railway at Spittal. A class A4, in its short-lived green livery, is seen crossing the Royal Border Bridge with, presumably, the Up 'Flying Scotsman' in the late 1930s. Tweedmouth harbour (see page 63 et seq) is prominent in the foreground. The painting was one of many commissioned by the LNER to decorate the compartments of its carriages. (Water colour by SR Badmin, RWS / private collection)*

Title page caption. *A postcard to advertise the East Coast Route, prior to the First World War, shows NER class C6 No 1794 about to leave its train from Newcastle at Edinburgh Waverley. (James Armstrong Collection)*

Rear cover captions.
Top: *The signal cabin at Widdrington dated from 1910 and was a style N4 building, albeit with N3-type locking room windows. A new 38-lever frame and gate wheel were fitted in May 1960; the bricked-up window in the end elevation and the new locking room door from the platform appear to date from this time. The new frame was at the back of the building and a new stove and chimney were added at the front. The extra-long gates also protected the access to the goods shed. This photograph was taken on 30 March 1968, and shows the nameboards still painted in the former North Eastern Region's pleasing combination of white and tangerine with a black surround; gutters, fall pipe and door are picked out in oriental blue. Widdrington signal box would close in August 1980 but the base survives today as a relay room. (John M Boyes / Armstrong Railway Photographic Trust)*

Centre: *Class B1 No 61354 works the Oxwellmains - Alnmouth empties across Alnmouth viaduct on 12 March 1966. (John M Boyes / Armstrong Railway Photographic Trust)*

Bottom: *A Type 4 works a secondary passenger service past Alnmouth in the late 1960s. Note the white-painted fish van at the head of the train. Note too how dirty it is; BR's approach to wagon cleanliness did not endear it to those customers who despatched foodstuffs such as fish. (John M Boyes / Armstrong Railway Photographic Trust)*

Introduction and Acknowledgements

This book has been written by members of the North Eastern Railway Association to commemorate our fiftieth anniversary in 2011. When we were looking for a suitable subject, we found the line from Newcastle to Berwick (N&B) was the most obvious choice; it has never had a detailed history, and is even omitted from the David & Charles' *Regional History of North East England*. What makes the omission even more surprising is that it is one of the most interesting railways in the North East. The Alnwick Branch, Alnwick & Cornhill, Amble Branch and the private North Sunderland Railway all have ample volumes covering their history, so why not their main line? The Kelso Branch is the only one served by the N&B without its own book, but that is now addressed by Christopher Dean's concise account in Chapter 7.

Reports commissioned by the Government have not been too favourable to railways between Newcastle and Edinburgh. As early as 1840 a report considered that the East-Coast route via Newcastle was less useful than a West-Coast one via Carlisle; fortunately it was ignored. In 1963 the Beeching report did not propose anything too drastic for the line, although it was suggested that it should not 'be developed'. Soon after the report the North Eastern Region considered singling stretches of the N&B even though it had been totally

resignalled as recently as 1962. For a time, in 1964-5, the uncertainty was such that track renewals were carried out with good second-hand material recovered from lines closed following the Beeching cuts. In 1983, not long before the work to electrify the route was to be started, a report by a civil servant suggested that it should be closed completely. Eight years later the electrification was complete, and now, nearly two decades on, its future is very certain as an essential part of one of the most profitable railways in Britain.

The authors are grateful for the assistance given by Ms Leona White, Curator, Head of Steam, Darlington Railway Centre & Museum, and the staff of the National Archives, Kew, Northumberland and Tyne & Wear Archives, and in particular the North of England Institute of Mining and Mechanical Engineers (NEIMME), Newcastle.

Valuable information and help has been given by the following individuals: Dr David Addyman, James Armstrong, Robin Coulthard, Alan Davison, Mark Sissons, Neville Stead, Mike Wild, Claire and David Williamson and Alan Young. The signalling experts have been acknowledged at the end of Chapter 8.

Special thanks are due to John Teasdale for his care in formatting the book and his invaluable help with the selection of photographs.

(Bill Fawcett)

4

Chapter 1 : Early Schemes, 1835-1840

John F Addyman

Trunk routes to convey passengers or freight between Edinburgh and Newcastle, either by road or rail, would sensibly follow the coast to avoid difficult, hilly terrain. When Thomas Telford (1757-1834) was asked to consider improvements to the existing roads from Edinburgh to Newcastle in the early Nineteenth Century, he rejected the more direct, but hilly, road via Soutra Hill, Greenlaw, Coldstream and Wooler to Morpeth (the modern A68 and A697) in favour of the Berwick Road (A1). Even though the Great North Road was 14 miles longer, and 'nearly the whole needed to be re-made on fresh ground...being frequently unfit for wheel-carriages', it provided a fairly level route.[1] In contrast, the Coldstream route crossed the Lammermuirs at Soutra, almost 1,200 feet above sea level, and Rimside Moor, north of Morpeth, at 650 feet. Figure 1.1 gives the main contours of Northumberland; it will be seen that any deviation from the narrow coastal strip would present difficulties in building roads or railways. However, 20 years after Telford's survey, when railways were being seriously considered in the area, some promoters were still to be convinced that the longer coastal route was by far the best on engineering grounds.

In 1836, with the London & Birmingham Railway in the process of being built, other railways were authorized to extend from it as far as Leeds and York. Part of the Great North of England Railway (GNER), from York to Newcastle, was also authorized, and plans were being considered for a line from London to York via Cambridge and Lincoln. 1836 also saw proposals for a coastal railway from Newcastle either to Dunbar or just as far as Berwick, and one via Redesdale, Carter Bar and Melrose to Edinburgh. The coastal one, the Grand Eastern Union Railway, was proposed by Matthias Dunn (1788-1869), Robert Hawthorn (1796-1867) and John Dobson (1787-1865) and estimated to cost £800,000.[2] It took a fairly direct route, passing a little to the east of both Morpeth and Alnwick, but did not make all the concessions for the topography that would have become evident had it been surveyed in detail. The other route, surveyed by Joshua Richardson (1799-1886), tackled the most difficult terrain, and was condemned by George Stephenson (1781-1848) because of the engineering problems; the worst being 'a tunnel eight or nine miles in length through the Carter Fell ridge'.[3]

On 1 January 1825 the consultancy firm of George Stephenson & Son had been set up: 'That Geo. Stephenson and Robt. Stephenson shall take charge of pointing out, surveying, etc., all lines of Road, and all other works which the Co. may undertake and shall be provided with proper assistants at the expense of the Co.'[4] A number of well-known engineers served apprenticeships with the firm and a pool of very competent engineers worked for it until it was dissolved following George's death in 1848. In practice George and Robert (1803-1859) never worked together on the construction of a railway. George usually did the initial route planning, which he was extremely good at, and Robert followed as Engineer-in-Chief for the construction of the line using engineers from the firm as assistants. The initial planning for the line between Newcastle and Berwick was under George Stephenson's control, but its building devolved to Robert.

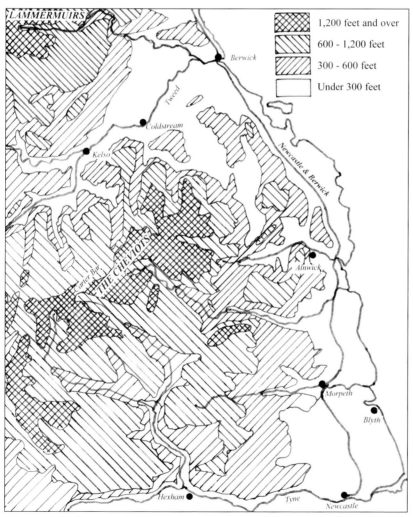

Figure 1.1. *A contour map of Northumberland and part of the Borders showing the disadvantages of any direct route through the centre of the county from Newcastle to Edinburgh. The Newcastle & Berwick Railway would reach a maximum height of 237 feet AOD at Cramlington. (JF Addyman)*

With his old enemy and former taskmaster,[5] Robert Hawthorn, proposing a railway north of Newcastle, it could not be long before George Stephenson was firmly in on the act. He had ended a report to the directors of the Edinburgh & Dunbar Railway Company dated 11 September 1836 with the words: 'I am convinced that if you can only obtain the Line as far as Dunbar, there will very soon be a locomotive communication between London and Edinburgh, along the east coast of Scotland and Northumberland.'

Great North British Railway

On 1 March 1839 plans were deposited for the Great North British Railway (GNBR) from Newcastle to Edinburgh with the leading Scottish railway engineers Thomas Grainger (1794-1852) and John Miller (1805-1883) responsible for the line from Edinburgh to Berwick, and George Stephenson & Son for the remainder. The GNER had plans to extend as far north as Newcastle's Town Moor, so starting the GNBR there would save it a lot of money and allow room for manoeuvring when the location and height of the bridge needed to cross the Tyne was finalized.[6] The means of crossing the river would tax engineers for another five years, and the final solution, by Robert Stephenson, would be a lot more expensive than anyone had bargained for. (See Chapter 4.)

The direct line of the GNBR, from its Town Moor start, was blocked by the Brandling family's Gosforth Park, and to avoid upsetting these powerful allies, George designed the route so it could pass either to the east or west of their grounds (Figure 1.2). The line then headed north-eastwards to a 'very favourable' crossing of the River Blyth near Bedlington Ironworks.[7] Immediately after crossing the Blyth, a 4½ mile branch headed north-west to serve Morpeth. George had explored all the country between the Great North Road and the coast and was convinced that to take the main line near Morpeth 'presented difficulties to a considerably greater extent than the Line near the Bedlington Iron Works.' Taking a straight line due north from Bedlington to Warkworth allowed gradients no steeper than 1 in 480, a minimum of earthworks, and 'the River Wansbeck to be crossed at a very favourable place', east of Warkworth. Sweeping curves took the line across the Aln immediately to the west of Alnmouth, where a deep cutting or very short tunnel would be needed (Figure 1.3). Three-and-a-half miles of level track took the line very near the sea past Howick, and it continued nearer to the coast than the present main line to Belford before taking a similar route to Tweedmouth.

The gradients and alignment proposed by George would have given a superb high-speed railway with a present day speed potential of over 140 mph for most of its length. George considered that the other advantages of the coastal route were that it would cross fewer roads, would suffer less disruption from snow, and would be ideal for moving troops in the event of an invasion.[8] The concrete relics of the Second World War that litter the coast show that his final point was not without foundation.

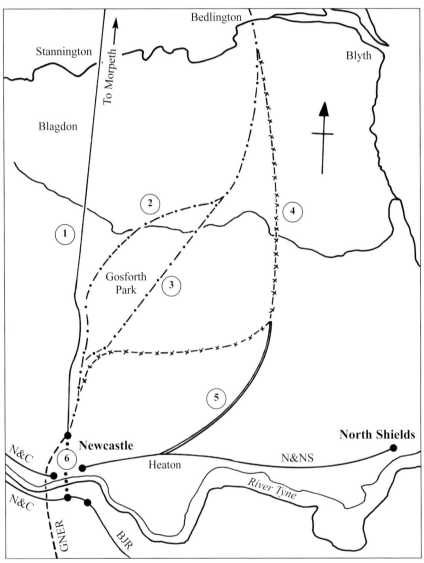

Figure 1.2. *Existing and possible lines north of the Tyne in 1839: (1) a direct line to Morpeth following the Great North Road as proposed by Dunn and Hawthorn, Bowman, Remington and, later, Brunel; (2) and (3) Stephenson's GNBR lines to the west and east of Gosforth Park as shown on the deposited plan of 1839; (4) an alternative proposed by George Stephenson in 1838; (5) Robert Stephenson's scheme to avoid tunnelling under Newcastle by using the N&NS from Heaton, which had opened in 1839; (6) the scheme to link the GNBR with the Brandling Junction if the GNER failed. (From a map in the possession of the NEIMME)*

The Newcastle & North Shields Railway (N&NS) opened in 1839 and had used viaducts with laminated timber arches, on stone piers, to cross the valleys of the Ouse Burn and Willington Dene. The estimated saving when compared with masonry superstructures was around £14,000 each.[9] He was so impressed by these that he proposed to use the same construction at least for crossing the Tweed and Tyne. Figure 1.4 shows part of the plan for crossing the Tweed with 11 laminated timber spans of 140 feet. By using timber throughout the total cost of the major viaducts was estimated at £250,000 – about the same as the final cost of the High Level Bridge over the Tyne.[10] However, unlike Locke and Brunel, Robert Stephenson was only prepared to use timber in structures as a temporary expedient – so the Newcastle & Berwick Railway was built with masonry and brick bridges.

Unfortunately, George's alignment upset a powerful landowner, Lord Grey, by daring to cross his 'Long Walk', or carriage drive, from Howick Hall to the shore. The Stephensons were reluctant to deviate from the original line, which passed more than half-a-mile from the Hall, and gave by far the best alignment and gradients. The story of this is and its damaging effect on the Newcastle & Berwick is given in Chapter 2.

Early Railway Proposals for Crossing the Tyne

When the GNER Act for the Darlington to Newcastle section had been granted in 1836, it had intended to approach the Tyne west of Gateshead, using the Team Valley, but it had not been decided whether to take the line near the bottom of the valley or maintain a higher, more easterly, course similar to the present East Coast Main Line (ECML). Thomas Storey (1789-1859), the GNER engineer, first proposed to cross the Tyne at a height of 74 feet near the site of the present Redheugh Bridge, and to extend the line northwards by means of a 1,000 yards long tunnel under Newcastle to reach the Town Moor. The bridge was intended to have two decks with the lower carrying the Newcastle & Carlisle Railway (N&C) tracks. It soon became evident to Storey that it was better to site the bridge further east, but this alienated the N&C 'who were desirous of holding the key to the approach to Newcastle'.[11]

1836 also saw an independent scheme by the Newcastle entrepreneur, Richard Grainger (1797-1861), with the assistance of the engineer Thomas Sopwith (1803-1879), 'for concentrating the termini of several railways near Newcastle upon Tyne'. Their line would have crossed the Tyne at a low level near the mouth of the River Team, exactly one mile west of the

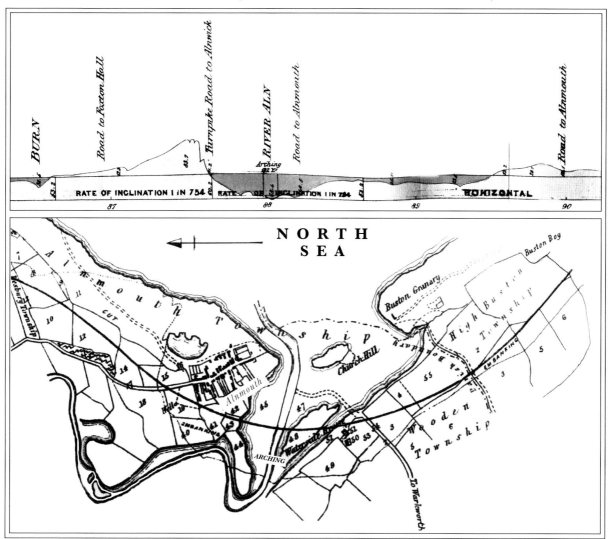

Figure 1.3. Above: the horizontal section at Alnmouth indicating the level or insignificant gradients on George Stephenson's original line. The deep valley of the River Aln would be spanned in part by a viaduct (marked as 'Arching' on the section). Below: the sweeping curves over the River Aln and past the village of Alnmouth.

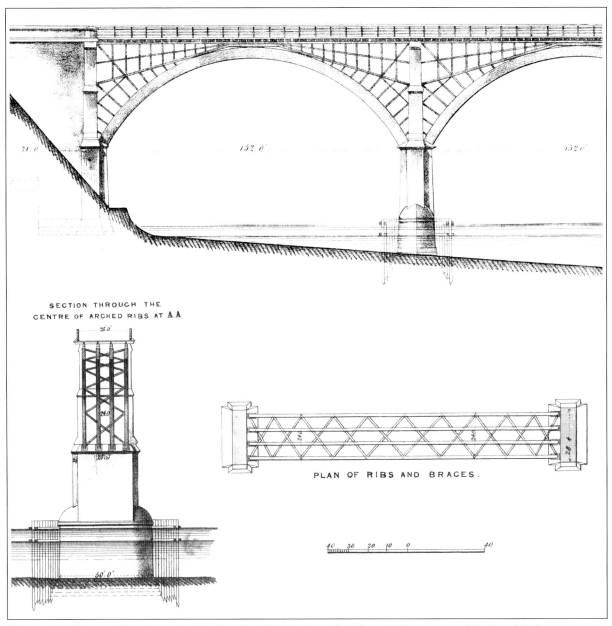

Figure 1.4. Plans and sections showing details of the laminated timber viaduct proposed by J and B Green to cross the River Tweed with eleven 140 feet spans. (Smith-Barlow Report, 1841)

site of the High Level Bridge. On the south bank of the Tyne it was intended to connect with the GNER from the south, the Brandling Junction Railway (BJR) from the east and the Newcastle & Carlisle from the west prior to the low-level crossing of the river. Immediately on the north bank was to be the depot, or station, where a main line headed due north for Edinburgh oblivious to the fact that the ground rose rapidly to 300 feet. From the depot two branches ran eastwards. One followed the river bank to serve Newcastle's busy quayside, and then climbed due north to connect with the proposed N&NS at Manors. The other was intended to serve central Newcastle by means of a rope-worked incline through a tunnel, which provoked the town council to put an end to low-level river crossings with inclines by resolving that 'the Tyne should be bridged at height that would allow railway companies to run locomotives into the centre of the town on any proposed route'; this also put paid to the N&C's low-level scheme.[12]

In 1837 with plans for the N&C's line from Scotswood Bridge, climbing along the north bank of the Tyne, about to be implemented, John Blackmore (1801-1844), the railway's engineer, now suggested a bridge at a height of 85 feet above the river. This would link the GNER in the Team Valley with the N&C's proposed depot, about half-a-mile west of the site of Central Station; there was no indication of any connection to a line to the north.[13]

George Stephenson, who was related to Thomas Storey by marriage, had been involved in the 1836 discussions about the revised site for the GNER bridge over the Tyne, and later must have known about that railway's difficulties in raising funds. This may explain why, from 1838, he included the cost of extending the GNBR through Newcastle in his estimate for the railway. If the need arose, he intended the GNBR to cross the river 'by a bridge, which must be sufficiently high to enable a junction to be formed on the opposite side with the Brandling Junction Railway'. His line, east of Storey's, would have run south from the station on the Town Moor and entered a tunnel 1,500 yds long before emerging from under Westgate Street. His description of the route from there to the bridge states:

> …it continues in open cutting on the south side of the old wall, until it arrives at the vacant ground adjoining the Forth, where an excellent station may be made for passengers. The line then passes under Forth Street, into the open ground adjoining Messrs. Hawthorn's and Messrs. Stephenson & Co.'s manufactories.[14]

Figure 1.5 is the plan produced by Harrison and Wood showing Blackmore and George Stephenson's crossings of the Tyne and possible links to all the proposed railways to the north and south.

Concurrently a plan was suggested by Robert Stephenson, to connect the GNBR with the Newcastle & North Shields Railway, at Heaton, in order to approach Newcastle from the east (Figure 1.2), thereby avoiding the tunnel and a steeper descent to a bridge over the Tyne. Fortunately the N&NS and the Brandling Junction, in Gateshead, were the same height above the river.

Darlington to Gateshead

George Stephenson had expected that progress could be made with the Newcastle-Berwick portion of the GNBR in 1841 even though 'we shall not be able to get money to go through the Town [Newcastle] at first but it is highly desirable that it should be brought to that part of the Town, where it can be carried forward to

Gateshead on the best possible plans'.[15] At this stage it was hoped that the GNER would reach Gateshead in 1842 or 1843 at the latest. However, when the GNER opened from York to Darlington in March 1841 it had no capital left to continue to Newcastle. Fortunately George Hudson (1800-1871), the 'Railway King', was to come into the picture with positive actions to complete the East-Coast line to Berwick, and assist with financing it thence to Edinburgh. Robert Stephenson had been brought in as Engineer-in-Chief of the GNER on 18 January 1841 following the delayed opening of the York – Darlington section caused by a bridge collapsing and other remedial work being needed. He quickly summed up the options for extending the line to the Tyne, and Hudson's powerful influence enabled the authorization and finance to be obtained rapidly.

A bold scheme of 1837 by TE Harrison (1808-1888) and Nicholas Wood (1795-1865), called the Northern Union Railway (NUR), was to disregard much of the GNER route north of Darlington, and link up railways, either built or authorized, east of the GNER, to form a cheaper alternative. They intended to use parts of the Clarence, Durham Junction, Stanhope & Tyne and Brandling Junction Railways to give less new construction but a 6 miles longer line from Darlington to Gateshead (Colour Plate 1 on page 19). A bridge over the Tyne from the BJR to N&NS at Bill Point, about 3 miles east of Newcastle, would allow an easy connection to a coastal line from Edinburgh.[16] (See Colour Plate 2 on page 20.)

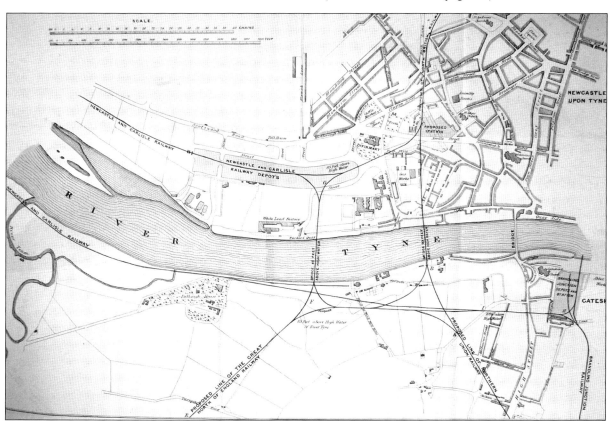

Figure 1.5. *A plan produced by Wood and Harrison in 1840 showing options for linking all the railways north and south of the Tyne. The proposed Central Station is on the north side of Neville Street. Blackmore's bridge (left) crosses the river 85 feet above high water and Stephenson's at 95 feet. The Northern Union is shown to cut through the centre of Gateshead to avoid a sharp curve at the BJR's station. (Smith-Barlow Report, 1841)*

Following the failure of the GNER in 1841 the Wood – Harrison scheme was reconsidered and it was decided to use neither the Clarence nor the Stockton & Darlington at the south end of the line but to build 24 miles of new railway to join the Durham Junction.[17] The GNER route, as far as Ferryhill, was subjected to some modifications, but then disregarded to use a new alignment, further east, to join the DJR south of its valuable Victoria Bridge over the Wear. A North Junction Railway was proposed by WA Brooks (1802-1877), with the intention of building five miles of new railway from the north end of the Victoria Bridge to join the BJR near Felling; this shorter route was not implemented until 1849. At this stage Hudson saved money by using the longer Stanhope & Tyne route to join the BJR further east, at Brockley Whins; Durham was served by a branch line. The line was completed on time and under budget, and the first train ran from London (Euston) to Gateshead on 18 June 1844.[18] Two weeks later the North British Railway (NBR) was authorized to build its line from Edinburgh to Berwick, which differed in some respects from the original GNBR plans. All that was needed now, to achieve an East-Coast route from York, was to devise a way of crossing the Tyne and to finalise the plans to reach Berwick.

The Smith-Barlow Report, 1841

Following a statement in Parliament on 19 May 1840, Sir Frederic Smith RE (1790-1874) and Professor Peter Barlow FRS (1776-1862) were required to produce the *Fourth Report on Railway Communication between London, Dublin, Edinburgh and Glasgow*. When it came out, in March 1841, it covered all the proposals to link the named cities, and gave arguments for or against the rival schemes to serve them. In 1840 it was already possible to reach both Lancaster and York from London (Euston), and by the time the report was issued the East-Coast route had reached Darlington. Surprisingly, their preferred route to Glasgow and Edinburgh was through the sparsely populated, mountainous districts, very similar to the present West Coast Main Line (WCML) via Carlisle. Fortunately this had little influence on the progress of the East-Coast lines.

On the east side of the country, north of the Tyne, they analysed four options (Colour Plate 1):

1. On considering the GNBR line, they felt 'Mr. Stephenson might, on further investigation, be induced to carry the East Coast Line nearer to Morpeth and Alnwick than originally intended'. They were not keen on using the N&NS for the final approach into Newcastle.
2. The 38-miles long Morpeth Deviation line, by Malcolm Bowman, was aimed to overcome objections in Morpeth caused by its only being served by a branch off the GNBR. It started on the Town Moor at the same point as the GNBR, but took a direct line to Morpeth, and then another direct line to join the GNBR south of Christon Bank. The acceptable gradients were achieved by earthworks 30% greater than on the GNBR, and the report thought that the extra expense was 'perfectly incompatible with any traffic that can

here be reasonably anticipated'.
3. George Remington's line via Morpeth, Wooler and Kelso to Dalkeith was roundly condemned: 'The cuttings, embankments and tunnels are of a formidable description, so much so indeed, that if no other Line were attainable, we would be reluctant to recommend this project'. The scheme included a five-mile long tunnel under the Lammermuirs at Soutra and a two-mile one under Rimside Moor.
4. John Blackmore proposed a line 'From Newcastle, by the Newcastle and Carlisle Railway, to Hexham, Note o' the Gate, and Galashiels to Edinburgh.' This line followed the North Tyne Valley to Kielder and then struck north over desolate and difficult country to pass four miles to the east of Hawick, but it made the impossible claim to avoid any gradients steeper than 1 in 165. The report had reservations about the long summit tunnel at Note o' the Gate (NT 589029) and that 'from Bellingham to Hawick there is scarcely any population'.

Later another line from the N&C to Edinburgh was proposed by George Johnson (1784-1852) and Nicholas Wood; both were colliery viewers and directors of the N&C. Their 1843 proposal ran from the summit of the N&C at Gilsland and made for Newcastleton in Liddesdale. It joined the Blackmore alignment near Melrose giving a line, from north of Newcastleton, very similar to that used by the Waverley Route, which opened 19 years later.[19]

Endnotes:
1. *Life of Thomas Telford* (Edited 1838) pp 250-2.
2. Prospectus 1836 Northumberland County Archives, SANT/BEQ/28/1/8. In 1835 Dunn and Hawthorn had proposed a 'circuitous' railway from Newcastle to Morpeth via Shankhouse with a branch to Blyth intended to serve the collieries. See also appendix to *Fourth Report on Railway Communication between London, Dublin, Edinburgh and Glasgow* (1841) (Smith-Barlow Report) p 80.
3. George Stephenson's report of 13 September 1838. Richardson's line was named 'Newcastle upon Tyne, Edinburgh and Glasgow Railway', and would have had branches to serve Kelso, Hawick and Selkirk. From Galashiels a direct route to Edinburgh followed the Gala Water, and another line serving both Edinburgh and Glasgow was proposed via Peebles. Even in the year that the Newcastle & Berwick was approved (1845) plans were deposited for a line via Carter Bar to Edinburgh. This was called 'Newcastle upon Tyne, Edinburgh and Direct Glasgow Junction Railway', and, more surprisingly, John Miller, who was currently building the NBR line from Edinburgh to Berwick, was its Engineer-in-Chief. The tunnel at Carter Bar was only to be $1\frac{1}{4}$ miles long but the line would have long gradients around 1 in 75. However, as Miller pointed out, in his report to the directors, these were no worse than those on other main lines, notably the Caledonian from Carlisle to Glasgow. Information supplied by Christopher Dean.
4. Quoted in Warren, JGH *A Century of Locomotive Building*, (1923 reprinted 1970) p 63.
5. Jeaffreson JC and Pole W, *The Life of Robert Stephenson*, (1864) p 60, quotes a letter from George to Joseph Locke's father in 1823 stating Hawthorn had been 'a great enemy to

me' some 20 years earlier.

6. Deposited Plans for GNBR, Tyne & Wear Archives.

7. The 1840's population of Bedlington, at around 3,200, was only 400 less than Morpeth, but, according to later NER figures, the population of its catchment area was about 50% greater. George's choice of a line near Bedlington, rather than Morpeth, seems sensible on all grounds.

8. George Stephenson's report of 13 September 1838 quoted in the Smith-Barlow Report.

9. Benjamin Green's paper on arched timber viaducts, *Proceedings of the Institution of Civil Engineers, Volume 5* pp 219-232. The one over the Ouseburn, which became part of the ECML, was to last for 30 years before it was replaced in wrought iron by TE Harrison.

10. Smith-Barlow Report.

11. Tomlinson WW, *The North Eastern Railway its Rise and Development* (1914 reprinted 1967) pp 294-5 and Deposited Plans.

12. Grainger's pamphlet and Newcastle Town Council Minute 9 November 1836.

13. Appendix to Smith-Barlow Report.

14. George Stephenson's report to Newcastle Committee of GNBR dated 19 November 1838.

15. Letter from George Stephenson 18 November 1840 quoted in Skeat WO, *George Stephenson : the Engineer and His Letters,* (1973) p 199.

16. Smith-Barlow Report.

17. Smith-Barlow Report. The S&D at Aycliffe, 6 miles north of Darlington, is only 1 mile west of the main line, but Hudson was set against using it.

18. Addyman J & Haworth V, *Robert Stephenson : Railway Engineer* (2005) pp 87-8.

19 Pamphlet on proposed railway 1843. NEIMME.

Figure 1.6. This is the title plate for the plans deposited on 1 March 1839 for the Great North British Railway, planned to connect Newcastle and Edinburgh by way of Berwick. In due course, the southern portion of this line would form the Newcastle & Berwick Railway.

Chapter 2 : The Routes

John F Addyman

Problems with the Major Landowners

Parliamentary Standing Orders for Private Bills required deposited plans and a book of reference containing the names of all the owners, lessees and occupiers of the lands that would be affected by the railway. In all, 780 acres of land were required between the point the N&B left the Newcastle & North Shields Railway and Berwick; this affected 269 landowners, 122 lessees and 435 occupiers. All three classes could be involved in the same piece of land, and their views were recorded as 'Assents, Dissents, Neuters or No Answers'. Of the landowners 100, accounting for 301 acres, were in favour, while 33 owning 255 acres were 'dissents'; the 'neuters' owned 58 acres and the 'no answers' 166 acres.[1] Once the Act was granted the railway company had compulsory purchase powers for the land it needed, so any opposition by landowners had to be made during the passage of the Bill through Parliament. Successful opposition could result in a year's delay while alterations to the scheme or payments to the greedy landowners were negotiated. Robert Stephenson had bitter memories of the defeat of the London & Birmingham Bill in 1832, in the House of Lords, by a resolution of Lord Brownlow (1779-1853) in support of the dissident landowners. Many railway projects had failed completely at this hurdle or had been forced to make alterations, as on the N&B,

which are detrimental to the travelling public to this day.

A formidable opponent to the railway, on purely selfish grounds, was the second Earl Grey (1764-1845). He had been Prime Minister from 1830 until 1834, and it was under his leadership that the famous 1832 Act for electoral reform had been passed. The Grey family had lived at Howick, about four miles north of Alnmouth, for over 500 years, and their old fortified dwelling had been replaced by the present house during the 1780s. In 1839, when Earl Grey's prospects of a peaceful retirement seemed to be endangered by the threat of a railway being built across a favourite part of his estate, his eldest son, Viscount Howick MP (1802-1894), took up cudgels on his behalf. Although the railway was to pass more than half-a-mile east of the house it crossed the 'Long Walk', or carriage drive, to the sea. When Sir Frederic Smith had examined the Stephenson line, in September 1840 'Lord Grey expressed very strong objections to a Railway passing through his pleasure-grounds, and cutting off his private communication with the sea'. When questioned by Smith, John Bourne (1811-1874), acting for George Stephenson & Son, had to concede 'that the Line might be changed to pass to the west instead of the east of Howick Park, by which means the inconvenience apprehended by Lord Grey might be obviated.'[2]

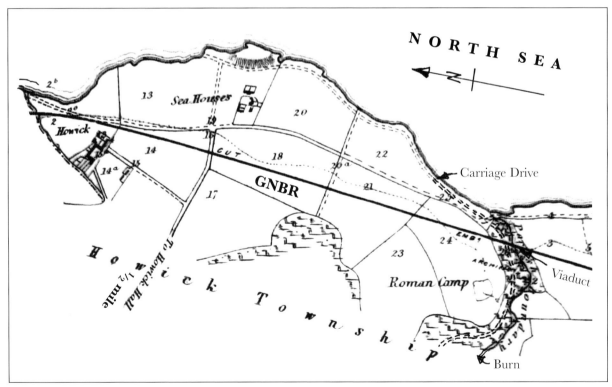

Figure 2.1. *Part of the 1839 deposited plan for the Great North British Railway (GNBR) showing the line running north from the Howick Burn to Howick village. The carriage drive, shown dotted, runs down the wooded valley of the Burn and then follows the coastline. After crossing a 396 feet long viaduct over the Burn and carriage drive the railway would have entered a shallow cutting through the agricultural land let to Grey's tenants. Howick Hall is more than half-a-mile west of the railway. The Burn was the boundary between the Duke of Northumberland and the Greys' land.*

The Stephensons hoped to avoid the diversion as it would give a worse alignment and increase the construction costs of the railway. Although a line to the west of Howick was no longer, the more difficult terrain that it passed through increased the cost by the equivalent of building two additional miles of railway.[3] George Stephenson wrote to his friend, Michael Longridge (1785-1858), on 30 November 1843 expressing his frustration at Grey's objections. He knew it was untrue that the railway ran through their 'pleasure grounds' as the land it was to pass over was arable and let to Grey's tenants. There was already a public road between the house and the intended railway, and the private carriage drive, which was largely hidden in the wooded valley of the Howick Burn, would be crossed by a viaduct; see Figure 2.1.[4] He felt the line to the west of the house would require a mile-long tunnel; this was later to be avoided by raising the line 120 feet higher, using long gradients as steep as 1 in 150 and heavier earthworks. He suspected an ulterior motive for the request to move the line west was that it would put the Greys' limestone quarries on the main line. He even went as far as to make a personal offer to the Grey family; 'we would cover the [rail]road in altogether; in passing the objectionable ground'. This tactic had been used elsewhere to overcome resistance of similar plutocrats on sensitive lengths of railways. After he had failed to get any agreement his private opinion of the Greys, as expressed to Longridge, was pungent:

> My senses are puzzled in judging how these people can set about making such paltry objections. It is compensation they want, nothing else... We shall not fear Lord Howick's opposition. Is the great thoroughfare through England and Scotland to be turned aside injuriously, for the frivolous remarks made by Lord Howick? No! the times are changed. The legislators must look to the comforts and conveniences of the Public. Are hundreds and thousands of people to be turned through a tunnel merely to please two or three individuals? I wonder their pulse does not cease to beat when such imaginations enter their brains. These failings are not becoming human beings. I can have no patience with them. However I suppose we must bend and keep our tempers until we get what we want.[5]

When Hudson took control he preferred to carry out negotiations with major landowners himself, and initially tried to ignore the Greys' unreasonable objections in order to preserve the better alignment and avoid the extra costs. George Stephenson was right in saying that Parliament had reached the stage where it was no longer possible for a prominent landowner to make a plea against a railway Bill on the grounds of personal inconvenience, so the very flimsy objection would be overruled. Howick knew this, and his only option was to go to the extreme length of promoting a rival company from Newcastle to Berwick, which

would pass to the west of his home.

In July 1844, after Hudson and the Stephensons had continued to refuse to alter their line, a provisional committee was set up to promote the rival Northumberland Railway to be worked by atmospheric power (see Chapter 3). The main supporters were Howick (chairman), WA Wilkinson (vice-chairman) and seven MPs either representing Northumberland or atmospheric interests. Wilkinson was chairman of the London & Croydon Railway, which was about to convert to atmospheric working, JL Ricardo, MP for Stoke, was very interested in the possibilities of atmospheric working, and Hananel De Castro was a trustee of the atmospheric patent holders; supporters included other landed gentry and the current mayor of Morpeth. The engineer chosen was Isambard Kingdom Brunel (1806-1859) who was at that time deluded by the possibilities of atmospheric propulsion.[6]

The other major landowner was Hugh, the third Duke of Northumberland (1785-1847), who owned one-fifth of the land that the railway intended to cross, and Hudson could not afford to upset him at this stage. The Duke was very concerned about his 'tentale' rents, which were raising him between £5,000 and £7,000 each year from the coal carried to the Tyne over the waggonways south of Morpeth, being lost to the main line when it opened. (A 'ten' was an archaic measure of $17^1/_2$ Newcastle chaldrons of 53 hundredweights giving 46 tons $7^1/_2$ cwts or 47.12 tonnes.) A draft agreement of 18 November 1844 included: 'Mr. Hudson for the Company undertakes and agrees to pay the said Duke his Heirs and Assigns; the same amount of wayleave tentale Rent, as if the same had been conveyed over His Grace's Estate.'[7] The Duke's solicitors were not too happy about a settlement with Hudson, and wisely sought counsel's opinion.

Counsel knew 'The House of Commons is extremely jealous of everything relative to coals, which may by possibility have the effect of enhancing the price, or destroying competition by which the price may be reduced', and felt the agreement, although the best way forward, could not 'be represented as being totally valid, such an agreement having been considered open to objection as being contrary to public interest'.[8] He cited cases, in Yorkshire, involving Lord Howden where similar measures had failed. Nevertheless a deed of covenant, covering the tentale rents and other matters, was signed by the Duke and Hudson on 26 April 1845.

Most of the collieries had direct access to the Tyne via existing waggonways, and it was stated in the Parliamentary evidence that the N&B would only carry 90 tons of coal per day. Needless to say Hudson did not honour the agreement to pay the equivalent rents from Netherton Colliery (south of Morpeth), and actually carried some of its coal over his own lines, not to the Tyne, but to Wearmouth Dock, which he had recently purchased.[9] This provoked Hugh Taylor, the fourth Duke's mining agent, to end a letter to Hudson on 19 April 1849 with 'I take it for granted it is not your intention to carry out the wayleave treaty with His Grace.' By this date Hudson's other dubious practices had been exposed and he was on his way out. A letter from Taylor to the Duke, dated 1 April 1850, stated the Hudson agreement was:

> … of trivial importance, not only from the small quantity of coals led, but because I have reason to believe, that the Owners of Netherton Colliery will very soon leave the Newcastle and Berwick line at Cramlington, and pass over Your Grace's Estate, and ship their coals in the Manor of Tynemouth.[10]

The Northumberland Railway was not without its implacable opponents. Sir Matthew White Ridley (1807 1877), who lived at Blagdon Hall five miles south of Morpeth, was firmly against Howick's line. He spent much of his year at Blagdon and was carrying out a series of improvements to the estate; and felt:

> It is not impossible that I may be so annoyed by this Railway as to lessen my desire to be as much here as I have been, and if the amount expended by me in various ways in this neighbourhood be in any material way diminished by my employing fewer people, it would be a serious loss to the population of this particular Locality.[11]

The Routes

In early July 1844 after Hudson learnt that Howick's idea to promote a rival Bill was 'no idle boast' he had the N&B alignment altered to pass west of Howick Hall; he informed the Greys that he had done so in a letter dated 1 August. Howick's explanation for still continuing with the Northumberland Railway was:

> This concession came too late: Mr. Brunel had consented to give his invaluable services as our Engineer, and the Gentlemen who had given me the most assistance had agreed to do so only on the express condition that the undertaking was to be a bona fide one, and once entered upon was not to be lightly abandoned: it was impossible for me to break faith with those who had so handsomely assisted me, and I could only tell Mr. Hudson that the time was gone by in which I should have been glad to accept his overture.

Hudson backed the Stephensons until the end of June 1844 when it became apparent that Howick really was to promote the rival scheme:

> It is true that such was the original design of Messrs. Stephenson that they honestly believed a line in that direction to be the best for the public, and not calculated to affect in an offensive or injurious manner the private rights or property of any individual. From the first moment that I became acquainted with the strong feelings of Lord Howick upon that point, I did not cease to urge Messrs. Stephenson to reconsider their plans; and my letter to his Lordship, of 1st August,

> was written on the very day that I learnt from them that a line might be carried in such a direction as to obviate his Lordship's objections.[12]

When Brunel wrote to Robert Stephenson in March 1845 to ask if any settlement was possible with Howick, prior to the Parliamentary contest, Robert offered a further explanation 'I fear Lord Howick and he [Hudson] have so misunderstood each other that a reconciliation will be difficult. Temper has in this instance, like many others stepped in, and to all appearance is riding roughshod over reason.'[13]

The Howick-Brunel and Hudson-Stephenson routes differed considerably over the first 25 miles north from Gateshead. (See Colour Plate 2 on page 20.) Brunel intended to use Hudson's new Gateshead station to start his 'Gateshead Branch', which would then cross the Tyne about half a mile upstream before turning east to terminate at the site of the present Central Station. He did not show connections to the N&C or N&NS railways at this point. In order to continue north the trains would have to reverse and negotiate a very sharp curve before plunging into a 2,410-yard tunnel under central Newcastle. Once clear of the town the line kept near to the Great North Road almost as far as Morpeth (which was to be served by a short branch) where it started to take a more easterly course eventually to follow close to Stephenson's revised line from Widdrington to Berwick.

Robert Stephenson proposed to leave the Brandling Junction before it reached Gateshead station, cross the Tyne with a high-level bridge and provide a joint central station with the N&C on a similar site to Brunel's on the south side of Neville Street. Trains to Edinburgh would again need to reverse and cross a long viaduct to join the N&NS for one-and-a-half miles from Manors to Heaton. The line then swung due north, well to the west of George's original route, and at Cramlington (where the proposed branch to Blyth left the main line) turned north-westwards to follow the Great North Road to directly serve Morpeth. After crossing the Wansbeck, unlike Brunel's, it diverted eastwards to miss the higher ground blocking its direct path. Both railways were to provide a branch to Kelso (see Chapter 7).

Serving Gateshead and Newcastle

As soon as the 1844 plans for the N&B had been deposited, suspicions were raised in Gateshead and Newcastle by Hudson's willingness to abandon Gateshead station, which was less than six months old, and the fact that he was prepared to pay £100,000 towards the cost of the Greens' proposed high-level, laminated timber, *road* bridge over the river (Figure 2.3). A railway across the Tyne and through Newcastle would be extremely expensive and, to prevent Hudson from altering the plans to a cheaper option, the councils insisted on safeguarding the railway through the towns. Had there been no competing railway the bridge could easily have been at Bill Point (see Colour Plate 2) resulting in both towns being served by branches off the main line.

In February 1844 a number of Newcastle councillors were quite happy for this to happen, and the mayor, Sir John Fife, said: 'It is in the interest of a large town like that [Newcastle] to have as many termini in or as near as possible; *and not that continuous lines should pass through it.'*[14] Almost a year later, the council had come to a very different conclusion and welcomed the plan 'to unite all the railway stations in one place near Neville Street.' But they were still not satisfied; Hudson was asked to attend a meeting in Newcastle, on 8 January 1845, where he was forced to agree to the road deck on the High Level Bridge and that:

> A clause shall be inserted in the Act by which the Newcastle and Berwick Railway Company shall be prevented from taking toll on any part of their line unless the bridge over the Tyne, and the passage of the railway through Newcastle, be completed within five years from the passing of the Act.[15]

These concessions were needed to get both towns' support to the N&B Bill, but the cost of the bridge, its approaches and Central Station was to be over half-a-million pounds – about one-third of the total cost of the railway. However, with most of the local MPs supporting Howick's Northumberland Railway, Hudson could not afford to take any chances which would lead to the Newcastle & Berwick's defeat in Parliament. Brunel building what the Stephensons knew to be an unworkable atmospheric main-line in their home county was unthinkable.

Serving Morpeth and Alnwick

As George Stephenson had discovered in 1838, Morpeth (population 3,800) was badly placed to provide an easily-graded main line to serve it, and this was backed up by the Smith-Barlow Report's comments on Bowman's Morpeth Deviation line (see Chapter 1). Brunel's line struck north after crossing the Wansbeck with a gradient of 1 in 100 and cuttings up to 30 feet deep through what the Stephensons knew to be hard rock. The Stephensons would have liked to have taken a straight line from Cramlington to north of Morpeth avoiding the town and reducing the length of the railway by two miles as shown in Figure 2.2. Robert Stephenson had famously bypassed Northampton when building the London & Birmingham, the North Midland had missed Sheffield and the line from York to Newcastle had avoided Easingwold, Thirsk and only served Durham by a branch.

Morpeth had raised protests, in January 1837, against Dunn and Hawthorn's line to Dunbar, and started its fight to be served by the current proposals as early as September 1844, when a petition of over 150 signatures was raised in the town. It is a measure of the strength of the opposition that the N&B main line was diverted, and the very sharp curve inserted, just to be as close to the town as Brunel's branch line. On 9 April 1845 the revised Stephenson line was accepted at a special council meeting as 'being of great advantage to the inhabitants of this borough', whereas Brunel's 'gives little or no public accommodation and will be

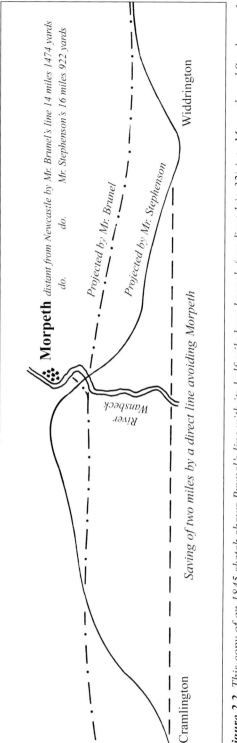

Figure 2.2. *This copy of an 1845 sketch shows Brunel's line with its half-mile long branch (gradient 1 in 32) into Morpeth and Stephenson's route distorted to come equally near to the town by using the very sharp 90° curve. The ideal line (bottom) would have missed Morpeth by over three miles and reduced the journey from London to Edinburgh by two miles. (Original sketch: NEIMME)*

highly injurious to this borough, and that this Corporation do therefore oppose it by every means in their power'. Their MP, Captain Frederick Howard, was requested to oppose the Northumberland Bill and support the N&B on behalf of the town.[16]

Contrary to popular opinion it was not the Duke of Northumberland who prevented the main line from directly serving Alnwick, but engineering difficulties. A railway following the line of the Great North Road from Morpeth to Alnwick would have encountered higher ground giving much steeper gradients than one nearer the coast. As explained in Chapter 6, the best solution was to serve Alnwick with a branch off the main line near Alnmouth.

Other Proposed Branches

The N&B's seven-mile branch from Cramlington to Blyth was authorized on the same day as the main line, and a two-and-a-half-mile branch off it to serve Bedlington was approved in the following year; neither was built. In 1846 the N&B deposited plans for an 'East Coast Line' with several starting points along the Tyne between Percy Main and Tynemouth, and joining the main line at Longhirst, north of Morpeth; it would have had branches to Seaton Sluice, Bedlington Ironworks and Blyth. (See Colour Plate 3 on page 21.) However, the Seghill Railway from Percy Main, which had opened in 1841, was being extended to reach Blyth in 1846, and in the following year it became known as the Blyth & Tyne Railway (B&T).[17] With most of the collieries in the area south of Morpeth and Blyth already being well served by waggonways or the B&T, and with the question of compensation to the Duke and other landowners for the loss of wayleaves, the N&B decided to abandon the idea of branches to Blyth. It concentrated on a line further north from Chevington to the newly improved Warkworth Harbour (Amble), at the mouth of the River Coquet, for which it had obtained Parliamentary approval in 1846.

In 1848 the York, Newcastle & Berwick (YN&B), as the N&B had now become, deposited plans for a half-mile-long-branch from Bilton station to serve Alnmouth (Figure 6.7, page 56), and a 4-mile-long-branch running west from Beal station to the Wooler-Berwick road, now B6525, near Barmoor (NU 003411). The latter had been agreed by Hudson during his negotiations with the Duke of Northumberland, but he may have had an ulterior motive for promoting the line. A very significant clause in the Barmoor Bill was:

> ...it would be attended with local and public advantage, if power were given to the said company to subscribe to the Sunderland Docks, authorised to be made by the Sunderland Dock Act, 1846; and the York, Newcastle and Berwick Railway Company are willing to execute the said proposed new works, and subscribe to the said Sunderland Docks.

George Hudson as MP for Sunderland was desperate to raise money for the new dock there by any means possible, and probably had no intention whatsoever of building the Barmoor Branch.[18]

The Amble Branch was inspected by Captain Laffan on 16 July 1849 on behalf of the Board of Trade, and considered to be unfit for passenger traffic; it was to be another 30 years before the NER got round to making the alterations necessary for passenger trains to run.[19] In 1873, just before the B&T became part of the NER, it deposited a plan for a nine-mile-long line from the Newbiggin Branch, near Hirst, to make an east-facing connection with the Amble Branch near Broomhill Colliery; its route took it within half-a-mile of the main line near Widdrington.[20] This proposal had its roots in the early 1860s, when the B&T Newbiggin Branch (opened 1872) was planned. The reason for reviving it, so late in the B&T's independent existence,

is a mystery. However, it may have provoked the NER to provide the belated passenger service to Amble, which opened from Chevington on 2 June 1879.

In November 1874, soon after the B&T take over, the NER deposited plans which included a number new connections between the two companies' lines. The most significant to this history was a proposal to link the N&B main line at Manors with the former B&T terminus at New Bridge Street, and then provide a further link from the B&T at West Jesmond to the main line at Killingworth.[21] Diverting East-Coast services on to this route could have considerably reduced the congestion caused by main line and Tynemouth trains using the same two tracks from Manors to Heaton, and cut the distance from Newcastle to Edinburgh by one mile at the expense of steeper gradients.[22] Neither scheme was pursued, and it was not until 1909, five years after the North Tyneside electric service had been introduced, that the essential link between New Bridge Street and Manors was opened; this allowed these trains both to start and finish at Central Station.

Endnotes:

1. Report of House of Commons Committee, 30 May 1845 Appendix E.

2. Smith-Barlow Report, page 23. George Stephenson's letter 8 September 1840 delegates meeting Smith to T Grainger and J. Bourne as quoted in Skeat WO, *George Stephenson; the Engineer and his Letters* (1973) p 198.

3. Robert Stephenson quoted an extra £30,000 in his House of Lords evidence on N&B Bill in June 1845.

4. Deposited Plans of GNBR in Tyne and Wear Archives.

5. Skeat, *op. cit.* pp 199-200.

6. Northumberland Record Office, Woodhorn, SANT/BEQ/ 28/1/8.

7. Letter signed by George Hudson 18 November 1844. NERA Collection.

8. Conservationists will be pleased to know that Parliament was far more concerned about protecting fishing rather than revenue from colliery wayleaves. When the Act for the Warkworth Harbour (Amble) Branch was granted on 16 July 1846 more than a page was devoted to ensuring that the Duke's salmon fishing on the River Coquet did not suffer during the railway or harbour's construction. There is a copy of the Act in the library of the Literary & Philosophical Society, Newcastle.

9. The Newcastle & North Shields Railway was not permitted by its Act to carry coals, so probably Monkwearmouth was the nearest available outlet for Hudson.

10. Papers relating to agreement between Hudson and the Duke. NERA and Northumberland Estates' Archives, also RAIL 506/5. The amount of coal travelling south from Netherton would indeed be small, as one of its two waggonways took coal in a north-westerly direction to Morpeth and the other north-east to Bedlington. An indication of the amount paid in wayleaves to the Duke is that the NER continued to pay 5 shillings (25p) per ten of 'Coals Coke Culm or Cinders,' carried on former B&T lines across his land.

11. Undated letter *circa* April 1845 from Sir MW Ridley. RAIL 506/8.

12. Extracts from long statement by Howick dated 14 October 1844 and counter-statement by Hudson dated 22 Oct 1844. The truth lay somewhere in between! RAIL 506/8.

13. Letter from Robert Stephenson dated 21 Mar 1845.

14. *Proceedings of Newcastle Town Council 1844*, 7 February 1844, p 39.

15. Letter from Hudson to the town council dated 9 January 1845 written after consulting Robert Stephenson about the road deck, which cast the die for the High Level Bridge as we know it.

16. Northumberland Record Office, SANT/BEQ/28/1/8.

17. The B&T Act of incorporation was passed in 1852, Tomlinson pages 510-1, 520. Therefore, most surprisingly, Joseph Locke and John Errington deposited a plan in 1852 for a line from North Shields to Morpeth via Bedlington Ironworks with a branch to Ashington. SANT/BEQ/28/1/8.

18. Evidence to the Committee of Investigation of the YN&B,

following Hudson's exposure, dated 19 July 1849, page 4.

19. For further history see *The Amble Branch* by Bartle Rippon (2007).

20. Northumberland Record Office, Q/R/UP/134.

21. Northumberland Record Office, Q/R/UP/136. This Bill also included the Tweed Dock Branch, see Chapter 6.

22. In 1900 the NER had powers to build a west to north curve connecting the former B&T and N&B at Benton, but, although they installed the signalling at that time, the loop was not built until World War 2 as part of an emergency diversion in case the main line was damaged by German bombs.

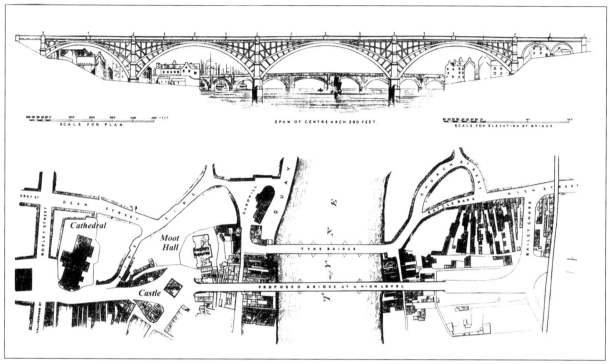

Figure 2.3. *These drawings show John and Benjamin Green's 1839 design for a high-level road bridge spanning the River Tyne, with Robert Mylne's masonry bridge of 1781 in the background. (Tyne & Wear Archives)*

Figure 2.4. *Bedlington was the first ironworks to roll wrought-iron fish-bellied rails, and was important enough to be considered in a number of early railway proposals besides the GNBR. (Author's Collection)*

Chapter 3 : Authorization

John F Addyman

Atmospheric versus Locomotives

The idea of moving vehicles by a piston fitted into a tube between the rails, in which a partial vacuum had been created, was first tried in 1840 by Samuel Clegg and Jacob and Joseph Samuda. The arm that connected the piston to the vehicle had to pass through a slot in the top of the tube, which was normally sealed by a greased leather flap, and the vacuum was created by large pumping engines spaced two to three miles apart. In 1843 when the $1^3/_4$-mile extension to the Dublin & Kingstown Railway had been opened to Dalkey with atmospheric propulsion it was described as a 'wonderful and extraordinary development.' It was welcomed by some very intelligent people as a sort of 'philosopher's stone' that could transform railways, and a number of companies considered its use.

After Robert Stephenson had been asked to prepare a report on the possible use of atmospheric power on the Chester & Holyhead Railway (C&HR) he examined the Dalkey Railway. His detailed report to the directors of the C&HR, of 9 April 1844, condemned the general use of atmospheric power as 'not an economical mode of transmitting power, and inferior in this respect both to locomotive and stationary engines and ropes', but he did concede that it might 'be applicable to a few short lines.' His father, Joseph Locke, JU Rastrick, GP Bidder and Daniel Gooch, the Great Western locomotive superintendent, supported this view, whereas IK Brunel, William Cubitt, Sir John Macneill, JM Rendel, the Samuda brothers, Thomas Sopwith and Charles Vignoles were engineers in favour of the atmospheric system.

Lord Howick had become one of the converted when he was chairman of a Select Committee set up to consider the competing railways to Epsom. He explained:

> …when the question of which of these Bills would be adopted it turned very much upon the system of working Railways by atmospheric traction. The evidence brought before this Committee was such as to impress, not only myself, but the four gentlemen associated with me in the enquiry, very strongly with the advantages of that system.

He had found that 'the opinion of several most eminent engineers was most decidedly in its favour', but admitted that the sole one against the system was Robert Stephenson who was '*the only engineer that had personally examined it*'. However, his evidence was discounted when 'we thought we discovered very strong symptoms of that bias of his mind in favour of the locomotive system'![1]

In February 1845 PW Barlow (1809-1885) gave a paper to the Institution of Civil Engineers that was critical of the atmospheric system. In the following discussion IK Brunel coyly claimed he 'did not wish to appear either as a supporter of the atmospheric system, or as wishing to condemn it'. However, he 'was quite prepared to admit, that there were many situations to which the system, in its present state, was inapplicable; but, as a practical man, he clearly perceived the manner of remedying many of the alleged defects; and, without that feeling, he should have considerable hesitation in recommending its adoption.'[2]

Another critical paper was given to the Institution on 15 April 1845 by (Sir) George Berkeley (1821-1893), who had actually served his apprenticeship with Samuda Brothers. Most of the long discussion following the paper amounted to an argument between Robert Stephenson and Joseph Samuda (1813-1885). The latter's parting shot anticipated the success of the atmospheric system, soon to be in use on the Croydon Railway, where 'he expected to exceed the performances of the Locomotive Engine – Mr Stephenson on the contrary expected the failure of the system. A short time would judge between them…' It did![3]

Figure 3.1. The piston-carriage of an atmospheric train on the London & Croydon Railway showing the driver screwing down the brake. The tube can be seen between the rails in the foreground. A partial vacuum of around 7 to 8 psi below atmospheric pressure was the best normally achieved. ('Pictorial Times', 1846)

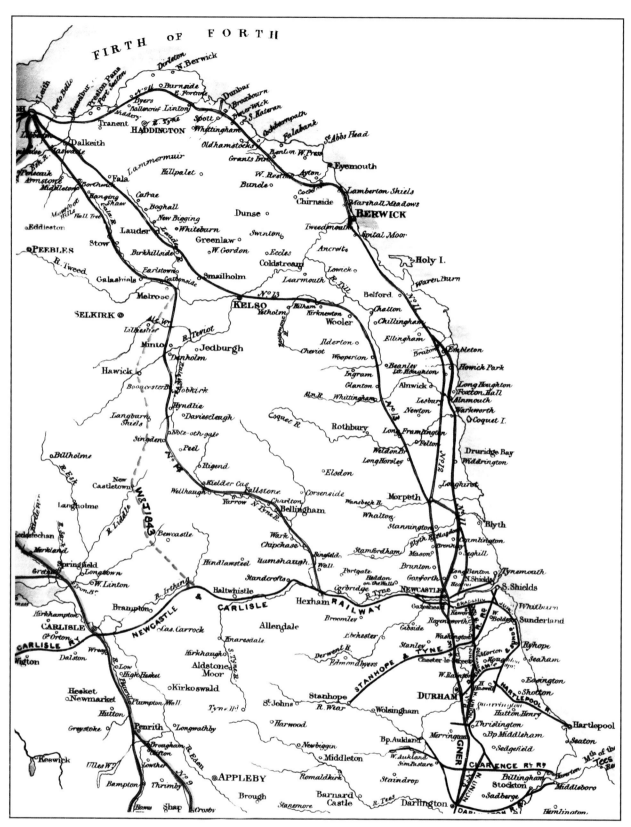

Colour Plate 1. *Part of the map from the Smith-Barlow Report showing existing and proposed railways between Darlington and Edinburgh; railways in use in 1841 are shown black. The original GNER proposal runs almost due north from Darlington to Newcastle passing to the east of Durham. The alternative by Harrison and Wood to join up existing railways is shown to the right of it. The preferred West-Coast line through Carlisle is bottom left. The 1843 N&C proposal from Gilsland to Edinburgh via Hawick has been added in orange, and John Blackmore's earlier N&C route from Hexham is line No 14. Both Bowman and Remington take a direct line from Newcastle to Morpeth (lines 12 and 13) before taking their less practical lines northwards. The GNBR (line 11) is shown as starting from either Newcastle or from Heaton on the Newcastle & North Shields Railway; note the Scottish section shows Dunbar served by a branch. (Smith-Barlow Report, 1841)*

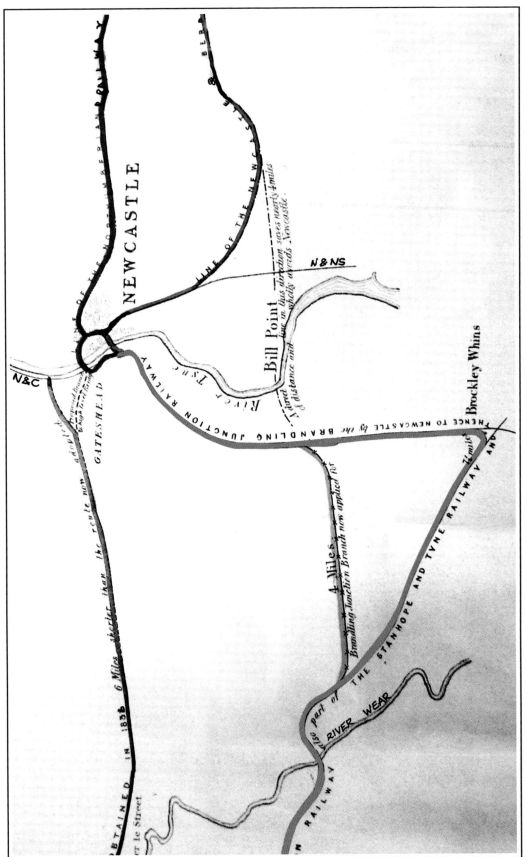

Colour Plate 2. *A plan produced in late 1844 showing existing and proposed main lines north and south of the Tyne. The green route is the one that came into use from Darlington on 18 June 1844 replacing the 1836 GNER Team Valley proposal shown brown (top left). When coupled with the yellow route (opened to passengers 1 October 1850) the very tempting Bill Point crossing would have allowed a considerable saving in distance and money. If Hudson had got away with this plan a triangular junction north of the river could have given connections into Newcastle via the Newcastle & North Shields Railway. The Brunel scheme is shown red and the final N&B scheme blue. (NEIMME)*

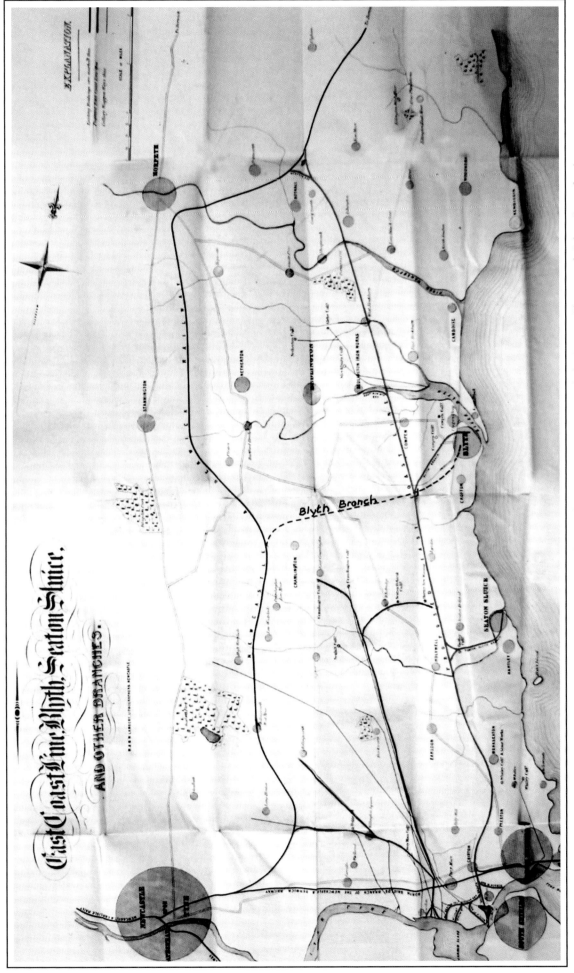

Colour Plate 3. *The aborted N&B scheme of 1846 for 'East Coast Line, Blyth, Seaton Sluice and Other Branches' (shown red) showing no less than five branches to shipping points on the Tyne between North Shields and Howdon.*

Colour Plate 4. (Left) Ouseburn Viaduct on the original Newcastle & North Shields Railway, drawn by JW Carmichael and engraved by W Collard. The railway was purchased by the N&B in 1845, and the viaduct was used as part of its main line from 1847. (Bill Fawcett Collection)

Colour Plate 5. (Below left) The Royal Border Bridge (Bridge No 195) seen from the north bank of the Tweed. The destruction of the ancient castle could not be blamed entirely or the railway companies as local residents had been removing its stone for years for use in the town's buildings. (JFA, 2002)

Colour Plate 6. (Below) Bridge No 5 on the N&B was inserted into the stone viaduct to provide a 60 feet span over the approach road from the High Level Bridge to central Newcastle. This spandrel-braced cast-iron arch was made by Abbot & Company of Gateshead. (Bill Fawcett, 2009)

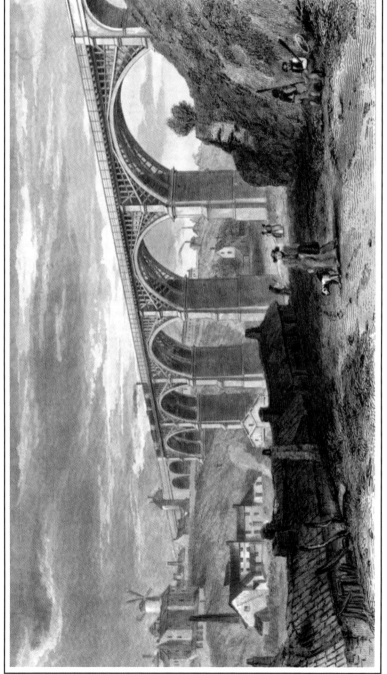

Brunel's South Devon Railway was authorized in 1844, and was intended to use the atmospheric power from the outset. However, the London & Croydon Railway, which had opened in June 1839, was having problems with locomotives on the three miles of 1 in 100 gradient at Brockley. The railway's management was convinced by Samuda Brothers that the atmospheric system would solve their problem.[4] The apparent superiority of atmospheric power on steep gradients was due to the fact that the *whole train* (25-30 tons) weighed less than the *locomotive* on a steam train. Furthermore, Robert Stephenson had to admit, in evidence to a Select Committee, that 15 coaches could be moved with the same power as that required just to move a locomotive and tender.[5] Five miles of the Croydon line was adapted to atmospheric working in January 1846, but the troublesome gradient was not converted until February 1847, just three months before the scheme was totally abandoned. However, in 1845, when the railways between Newcastle and Berwick were being considered, this expensive lesson still had to be learned.

In January 1845 the Board of Trade had reported against the use of atmospheric power on the London to Portsmouth line, and its February dismissal of the Northumberland line (see next section) led Samuda and Clegg to successfully petition Parliament to appoint a Select Committee on Atmospheric Railways. The report, which appeared on 22 April 1845, did not help either railway. The fact that the Prime Minister, Sir Robert Peel, was in very much in favour of the atmospheric system possibly influenced the committee's failure to condemn it outright for long, trunk railways: 'While Your Committee have thus expressed a strong opinion in favour of the general merits of the Atmospheric principle, they feel that experience can alone determine under what circumstances of traffic or of country the preference to either system should be given.' It was left for Select Committees on individual lines to find against the system thus causing extra expense and delays for the railway promoters. In mitigation no one disagreed that it appeared to work on very short commuter lines with frequent, light trains. The Croydon and South Devon lines ceased to use it in 1847 and 1848, but the $1\frac{3}{4}$-mile long Dalkey line continued with atmospheric power in the uphill direction until 1854.[6]

What happened on Brunel's South Devon Railway will give an indication of what would have followed had his Northumberland Railway been approved. When atmospheric working was abandoned on the South Devon it had only been extended over the 20, almost dead-level, miles from Exeter to Newton Abbot. West of Newton Abbot, where gradients were as steep as 1 in 36, it was worked by locomotives. Despite the incessant problems of keeping the continuous leather valve airtight, the frequent, light trains on the atmospheric section achieved a fair degree of reliability. The real problem that led to its demise was insufficient power for working heavier trains, leading to them having to be split and worked in portions. The perceived wisdom when the line was planned was that

13 inch diameter tubes would be satisfactory, and the capacity of the pumping engines was matched to this size. However, Brunel installed 15 inch tubes, and, just prior to the abandonment of the system, was casting 22 inch tubes to give almost three times the cross-sectional area of the first idea. The original pumping engines were already working beyond their design capacity, and much larger ones would be required to create the required vacuum in the 22 inch diameter tubes. If there was insufficient power on level section, how much more would be needed on the extreme gradients further west and how would the axles of vehicles and the fireboxes of locomotives have cleared this larger tube without modifications to the track? Any increase in power would mean more expense, and having spent £434,000 so far on the installation the directors decided to abandon the scheme, leaving the shareholders with a net loss of £350,000. It had operated on less than half the railway for just 51 weeks from 13 September 1847.[7]

The figures for the installation of the atmospheric system on the South Devon would suggest that considerably more than the *total* cost of the Northumberland Railway, quoted in its Bill, would have been needed *just to provide the equipment*. However, this was still to be discovered in 1844, and there was no intention to deceive. The *Railway Times* summed up Brunel: 'We do not take him for either a rogue or a fool, but an enthusiast, blinded by the light of his own genius'!

Reports and Decisions

In February 1845 the, now normal, report by officers of the Railway Department of the Board of Trade was published 'for the assistance of Parliament in forming a judgement' on the comparative merits of the N&B and Northumberland Railway schemes.[8] Although it came out in favour of the N&B it did not totally condemn the use of the atmospheric system. At this stage the projectors of the Northumberland line had every confidence in the atmospheric working, and felt it 'extremely improbable, that an unforeseen failure of an experiment now about to be tried on the Croydon to Epsom line, should compel them to resort to the use of locomotive engines.' The report sympathized with the claimed advantages of the system, so far proved on the Dalkey line, provided that all the mechanical difficulties could be overcome. With some foresight it pointed out that if locomotive working had to be introduced the gradients 'may become a formidable evil'. Some were as steep as 1 in 50 and there were 'upwards of five miles at an inclination steeper than or equal to 1 in 100, and of $8\frac{1}{2}$ miles of an inclination between 1 in 100 and 1 in 150.' The severe gradients on Brunel's South Devon line, which were never worked by atmospheric traction, as intended, present 'a formidable evil' for train working to this day. The report found that the provision of the superior gradients on the N&B had 'not involved any disproportionate increase of expense.'

The Achilles heel of the Northumberland Railway was it only being proposed as a single-line; 'the opinion of some eminent authorities has been strongly expressed to the effect that a double line, with double tube, &c. would be indispensable'. However, the capital quoted in the Bill for the Northumberland Railway was already £1,000,000, and that for the double-line N&B only £400,000 more. As the N&B was providing $8\frac{1}{2}$ miles of additional branches 'as well as much more complete and expensive passage of the Tyne and through the town of Newcastle' which was 'decidedly preferable' the report did not consider the extra cost unreasonable.

The Northumberland supporters claimed that 'their scheme is entirely independent of all existing Railway interests' and raised questions about 'a virtual monopoly among the different lines forming the Eastern line' from Rugby to Edinburgh if the N&B was authorized. The report disagreed and considered 'many of the important benefits of Railways to the community at large can only be obtained by uniting through-lines in one interest.' It would also 'enable them to contend, at the greatest possible advantage, with the competition of the Western lines for Scotch traffic.'

The report concluded that the N&B was 'decidedly the better line' as it was based on locomotive working 'which alone has undergone the test of experience'. It served the principal towns 'in a manner considered by the inhabitants to be more conducive to their interests', and 'it affords more convenient bridges across the Tyne and Tweed.' Its connection with other railways on the eastern line 'affords a better guarantee of its completion, and for it being worked in a manner the most beneficial for the public.' Earlier it had accepted that 'there would have been no likelihood of opposition to it [the N&B], had not the line as originally laid out threatened to interfere in a particular instance with private property in a manner considered so objectionable, that an opposition Company was got up for the express purpose of averting the injury.' However, it did not point out that the Stephenson line had already been modified, at some expense, to avoid the objectionable landowner.[9]

In May 1845 the N&B and Northumberland Bills were considered by a Select Committee of the House of Commons, where the two sides promoted their cases in 'a vigorous and determined manner'. By this time engineers had become very proficient in dealing with the questions posed by the opposing counsel, and could no longer be subjected to the mortifying experiences that George Stephenson had suffered in the 1820s. George Bidder, the Stephensons' friend, was particularly adept, and, on the technicalities of train resistance, was so fluent that the N&B's own counsel remarked; 'he had never been so puzzled at any examination since he had undergone the one preparatory to taking his degree at Cambridge'!

However, the case for locomotives was won, not on technicalities, but on practicalities. As was to be proved on the South Devon the size of the tubes and power of the stationary engines would be critical factors. The trains on the atmospheric system would generally weigh between 30 and 35 tons, whereas freight trains on locomotive lines already exceeded 300 tons. About 1,000 tons of freight traffic was expected to be carried over the line each day, and TE Harrison gave crucial evidence for the N&B in estimating that 44 trains would be needed to cover freight and the passenger traffic in *one direction* by the atmospheric system; when the N&B opened around 15 trains in each direction were all that was necessary.

Although speeds as high as 60 mph were claimed, the stopping and starting abilities of the atmospheric trains were disputed. The brake power of the piston carriage was very limited, and Brunel had had to extend the platforms on the South Devon as it was difficult to stop the train at exactly the right place. The time needed to recreate vacuum after trains had passed each other at the end of a single line section could be as much as 17 minutes. Both these factors would effect the overall journey times and totally negate any advantage of high intermediate speeds. Robert Stephenson had calculated that the stoppages on a single atmospheric track, if used on the busy 112-mile long London & Birmingham Railway, would have given journey times of 10 hours against under four with locomotives.

The operating inflexibility of a single line, not being able to reverse trains, the tube having to be broken to give access into passing loops, sidings or branch lines, and difficulties in dealing with accidents all stacked up against the atmospheric system. All shunting at stations would have to be by locomotives, horses or manhandling.

The atmospheric faction confidently stated that all the difficulties, real or imaginary, could be surmounted, but the Commons Select Committee did not agree in its decision of 30 May 1845:

> Your Committee do not feel called upon to express an opinion on the comparative merits of the Atmospheric and Locomotive systems, or on their comparative application to Railways in general. For, even assuming the efficiency of the tractive power under the Atmospheric system, and admitting the proposed Northumberland Line to be unobjectionable in an engineering point of view, still the evidence taken before your Committee does not justify them in coming to the conclusion that *a single Atmospheric line, with the arrangements at present in contemplation, can carry the estimated traffic between Newcastle and Berwick with the same convenience and punctuality which are already attained by the Locomotive lines of which it would be a continuation.*[10]

After the decision the editor of the *Newcastle Journal* expressed his relief and his gratitude to George Hudson:

> We are not sorry the investigation has taken place, for it has shown the utter inapplicability of the atmospheric system, as at present understood and developed, to a great trunk line; and, without inquiring into the motives in which the opposition to the locomotive

line projected by Mr Hudson originated, the public must consider they have been relieved from the infliction of a great and permanent evil by the decision of the Parliamentary Committee in this case. An enormous expense has been incurred, estimated at upwards of fifty thousand pounds, in defending a measure, the practical utility of which was never questioned, and after conciliation had done its utmost, without success, to appease the irritability of its pertinacious opponent. To Mr Hudson the inhabitants of Newcastle, and of "broad Northumberland," are deeply indebted, for, without his powerful aid, the trunk line north of Darlington would not have been yet extended to the Tyne, and, as to its progress northwards, there can be no hesitation in affirming that, but for the application of his gigantic mind to the subject, and the vast appliances which he, of all living men, alone could command, it must have remained in abeyance a lengthened and indefinite period.[11]

Four years later a much different view would be expressed about Hudson when it was alleged that he had 'illegally appropriated the sum of £184,204 of the funding of the York, Newcastle & Berwick Railway for his own use'.[12]

The Committee of the House of Lords sat during June and, having heard the N&B's case, concluded on 28th that they

> "…could not entertain an atmospheric line on its merits, but they would go into the case of [its being submitted as] a locomotive line, thereby placing both lines on their general merits." The counsel of the Northumberland Railway replied: "That being the case, my Lord, we shall not offer evidence. It would be wasting time after such a decision." The opposition to the N&B was therefore withdrawn and that of the landowners.[13]

For the Northumberland Railway to overcome the problems of handling the traffic, outlined by Stephenson and Harrison, it would have to be double track, and to do this with the atmospheric system would have cost over £3,500,000. When, inevitably and very soon, the line would have to be converted to locomotive working two-thirds of this capital would have been wasted. The Parliamentary Committees really did the promoters and subscribers a great favour by rejecting it. However, its opposition did cause a lot more expense to be incurred by the N&B to placate various interested parties, and resulted in a trunk railway being obliged to give fuller consideration to local needs rather than to economy, speed and directness.

The second Earl Grey died on 17 July 1845, less than two weeks *before* the N&B Act was passed, so his selfish objections gained him nothing at all.

Endnotes:
1. Howick's statement of 14 October 1844. RAIL 506/8.
2. *Proceedings of the Institution of Civil Engineers*, *Volume 4*, pp 146-7. PW Barlow was the eldest son of Professor Peter Barlow.
3. *Ibid*, p 289.
4. Hadfield C, *Atmospheric Railways*, (1967) pp 34, 213.
5. *Evidence to Select Committee on Atmospheric Railways*, pages120-1. NEIMME.
6. Hadfield, *op cit* p 213.
7. *Ibid*, p 172-6.
8. In 1844 WE Gladstone, as president of the Board of Trade, had set up a system whereby its officers would prepare a report on every deposited railway Bill. Parliament accepted the Board of Trade recommendation on 213 of the 245 Bills that it considered.
9. A *Report of Railway Department of the Board of Trade on the schemes for extending Railway Communication from Newcastle to Berwick* was completed in February 1845. NEIMME.
10. *Report from the Committee on the Newcastle and Berwick Railway Bill*, 30 May 1845. NEIMME.
11. *Newcastle Journal*, 31 May 1845.
12. *Ibid*, 18 July 1849.
13. *York Courant,* 3 July 1845.

Chapter 4 : Engineering the Line

John F Addyman

In 1845 the prospect of building nearly 100 miles of railway with several major viaducts was not a particularly daunting one. In his speech at his retirement dinner, in Newcastle station on 30 July 1850, Robert Stephenson contrasted the basic problems that had to be solved by principal engineers, in the previous century, with the current ease of carrying them out:

> Smeaton had not only to plan but to execute; he had to devise even the machinery and the apparatus by which the work was done.... The modern engineer has only to say, "Let this or that be done," and it was done. There were contractors with immense capital, and possessed of ample intelligence and skill for its direction, who would undertake the execution of any works, however difficult or stupendous.

The High Level Bridge[1]

The bridge over the Tyne was to present the greatest problems for Robert Stephenson. The first to be solved was the foundations for its piers as there was found to be between 20 and 50 feet of silt, some of it like quicksand, between the low water level and the bedrock. Fortunately even this problem could be solved more easily as James Nasmyth (1808-1890) had made

great step forward with his new steam piledriver, which had been introduced in 1845. This machine was capable of delivering 60 to 70 blows per minute to the heads of the piles compared with one blow every four minutes with the contemporary, hand-operated ones. The timber piles were 12 inches square and as 20,000 linear feet of them needed to be driven to support the bridge it meant, even with the Nasmyth machine, the pile-driving would take a year-and-a-half as an average of only around 40 feet could be achieved in a day. When the piles had been driven to their limit the battered heads were carefully cut off level and mortised to take the 12 inch square Memel sills which, in turn, supported two courses of 3 inch planking laid diagonally across the sills and at right angles to each other. This planking formed the base for the masonry of the piers: 'Such a foundation for so lofty a structure rendered it necessary that the whole design should be as light as consistent with safety.'[2] The height from high water level to the rails was about 110 feet, and it was as much as 60 feet below to the bedrock.

In order to fulfil conditions laid down by the Admiralty the spans of the bridge were fixed at 125 feet, and the piers were made as light as possible by means of arches and voids incorporated in their design. (Figure 4.1) For the superstructure, which is regarded

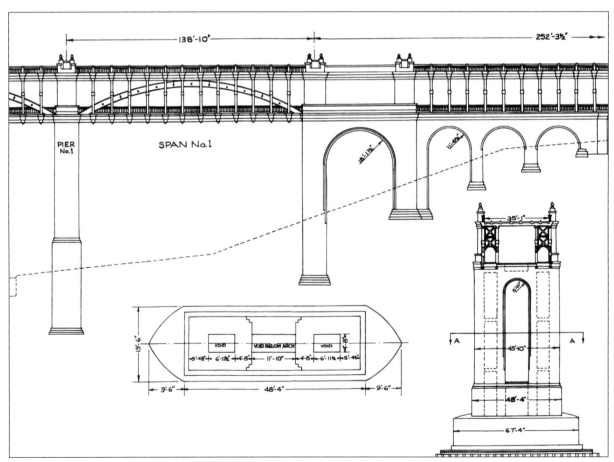

Figure 4.1. *This shows the Gateshead span of the High Level Bridge, the land arches and details of the piers. There were four cast-iron arches for each span, one on each side of the footways on the road deck; the footways were six feet wide, and the carriageway was 20 feet wide. (JFA)*

in its listing as 'one of the finest pieces of architectural ironwork in the world', Robert Stephenson adapted a design which he had first used on the London & Birmingham Railway over a canal in Northamptonshire in 1835 or 1836; this was a tied or bowstring arch with the deck suspended from the arch.[3] (Figure 4.2) On the High Level Bridge he suspended the road deck from the arches with wrought-iron rods, and supported the rail deck above it with cast-iron columns. The use of the bowstring arches meant that no thrust could be transmitted to the piers, and if slight settlement of the foundations occurred it would not affect the structural integrity of the bridge.

Figure 4.2. The original drawing of the tied arch with suspended deck as used over a canal on the London & Birmingham Railway in the mid-1830s. The ends of the arches were tied by wrought-iron rods extending below the deck. (Courtesy Ove Arup)

Contracts for the High Level Bridge were let in July and August 1846 – a year after the first contract for the line because of the amount of detailed design work required. The main contractor for the ironwork was Hawks, Crawshay & Sons of Gateshead who had submitted a price of £112,000. John Rush and Benjamin Lawton of York won the contracts for the bridge piers and land arches and for the Newcastle viaduct for £94,000 and £82,000 respectively; the short, Gateshead approach viaduct was let to Wilson & Gibson of Newcastle for £9,861.

Driving the piles to support the piers commenced in October 1846, and the first ironwork of the superstructure was placed on 10 July 1848; all was complete by 7 June 1849. The first passenger train crossed the bridge on 15 August and the road deck was opened to traffic on 4 February 1850. Earlier, the contractors' scaffolding on the east side of the bridge had been modified to become a temporary viaduct, and was opened on 29 August 1848, allowing trains to run through from London to Tweedmouth. The total cost of the bridge and its immediate approaches exceeded the tender price by 18%, but most of this was accounted for by the cost of the temporary viaduct and problems with the main foundations.

Of the three tracks on the upper deck, two were used by all trains and the western one was intended for northbound goods traffic; in practice the goods line was usually occupied by locomotives from Gateshead shed waiting to join their trains at Central Station. From the road deck's opening in 1850 until May 1937 all pedestrians, livestock and vehicles were charged a toll for crossing the bridge, and, until 1952, rail passengers paid the equivalent of an extra three miles fare for crossing it. These charges were permitted by the Act and meant the bridge was paid for over a relatively short period.

Carrying the railway on a viaduct over the east end of Newcastle raised questions at the House of Lords enquiry. Robert Stephenson had stated that it would cross Dean Street at about 70 feet and that the average height through the rest of the town would be 25 to 30 feet, and was asked: 'Do you see nothing objectionable in crossing a town at that elevation?' It had already happened elsewhere and he replied: 'No, it has not been found by experience to be so'. Although there are more than 40 spans many of them are so buried in the urban landscape that they are not even apparent. The fine cast-iron arch over St Nicholas Street (Colour Plate 6), on its approach to the High Level Bridge, and the elegant, much admired, 78 feet span arch over Dean Street are well known, but the arches over Pilgrim Street and Manor Chare pass unnoticed. (Plate 4.1) Had this 750 yards long structure been built with a more open aspect it would be seen in total as a very impressive piece of work.

Plate 4.1. Part of the Newcastle viaduct as it curves to cross over the Manor Chare before reaching Manors. (Bill Fawcett, 2009)

27

The viaduct was widened, mainly on the north side, in 1894 to carry two additional tracks; some arches were replaced in the late 1920s to allow the approach road to the new Tyne Bridge and more in the 1960s to accommodate the urban motorway.

Heaton to Berwick

The $12^3/_4$-miles Killingworth contract was let just two weeks after the passing of the Act, indicating that the plans and bills of quantities had been prepared well in advance of approval. It was let to Rush & Lawton for £90,000; they were later to win two contracts for the High Level Bridge. Three more contractors were successful on 1 October 1845. Richard Hattersley and his brother-in-law John Willans Nowell won the Morpeth and Warkworth contracts at a tender price of £233,400; their work, covering the $25^1/_4$ miles from Morpeth to Chathill, included the Wansbeck, Coquet and Aln viaducts.[4] Grahamsley & Reed were awarded the 11-mile Tweedmouth contract for £64,350. James McKay & John Blackstock won the $14^1/_2$-mile Belford contract for £87,550, and, a year later, the 1-mile contact that included the Royal Border Bridge for £184,000. McKay & Blackstock's contracts were unique on the line as they also included the erection of the railway buildings on the Belford length and Tweedmouth station was later added to their Royal Border Bridge contract.

The use of the Newcastle & North Shields Railway, as far as Heaton, meant that the problem of crossing the Ouse Burn had already been solved by John Green's five-span laminated timber viaduct. (Colour Plate 4)[5] At Plessey, $12^1/_4$ miles from Central Station, the River Blyth was crossed by five segmental arches of 50 feet span. Like all the following viaducts it had brick arches in an otherwise masonry structure. Bothal Viaduct over the River Wansbeck, one mile north of Morpeth station, had nine main arches of 50 feet span; its height above the river was over 120 feet. (Plate 4.4) The viaduct over the River Coquet, two miles south of Warkworth, is twice the height of the one originally proposed immediately east of the ancient town by George Stephenson, but it is only 600 feet long compared with his 1056 feet timber one. Again it had nine arches of 50 feet span and a maximum height of 90 feet. (Plate 4.3) The Aln Viaduct is 1,068 feet long, has 18 segmental arches and a maximum height of 75 feet. Poorer ground conditions in the valley of the River Aln meant that the spans of its viaduct were reduced to 30 feet; the river spans were on shale and most of the remainder on strong clay, but the first, fourth and northernmost piers needed piled foundations. (Plate 4.5)

Inspections of new railways had been started in 1840, but an Act in 1842 reinforced their authority by preventing any new passenger-carrying railway from being opened unless it had been inspected and approved on behalf of the Board of Trade (BOT). The inspectors were officers of the Royal Engineers, who were initially paid two guineas a day plus expenses.[6]

The first inspections on the N&B were carried out by Captain Joshua Coddington (1802-1853), but, after he resigned in 1847 to become general manager of the Caledonian Railway, two younger officers took over. Captain (later Lieutenant-General Sir Robert) Laffan (1821-1882) did the inspections for the High Level Bridge and the Amble Branch, while Captain (later Field-Marshall Sir Lintorn) Simmons (1821-1903) carried out those for the permanent viaducts over the Blyth, Wansbeck and Coquet, and the Royal Border Bridge.

Captain Coddington's reports of the line from Heaton to Chathill gave a description of the temporary viaducts used at the major river crossings, which were similar to those used by TE Harrison to span some broad valleys in County Durham.[7] The tops of the timber structures, which carried a single-track, were slightly wider than the intended masonry parapets and, for stability, their bases were a lot wider than the foundations of the piers. The arrangement of the spurs allowed the piers and the very shallow segmental arches to be built without obstruction, while the trains ran safely on the wooden deck above. Captain Coddington passed the Heaton to Morpeth section to open on 1 March 1847, with its temporary viaduct over the River Blyth. Chathill to Tweedmouth, without any major structures, was permitted to open four weeks later on 29 March. From 5 April four trains a day, in each direction, ran between Newcastle (Carliol Square) and Morpeth and Chathill and Tweedmouth, with coach services between Morpeth and Chathill and between Morpeth and Alnwick. There were also coaches between Tweedmouth and Berwick giving a total journey time from Newcastle to Berwick of nearly four hours.

The railway between Morpeth and Chathill presented more engineering problems; besides having three major viaducts there were some difficulties with the earthworks. Near Chevington it had its own little Chat Moss[8] where the ground was so soft that 'the contractor lost several horses which went down in it', and layers of brushwood and hurdles had to be laid to provide a firm foundation for the track. The 60 feet high embankment over the Brocks Burn, near Bothal (NZ 232877), was still moving, when Captain Coddington made his inspection, and the culvert over the burn was being extended to accommodate the slippage of the fill.

The inspection was carried out between 14 and 17 June 1847, and was a little premature. Besides the culvert at Bothal, the temporary Coquet Viaduct was not quite finished and the permanent Aln Viaduct still required fill above some arches to be completed and the track to be laid over it. The building of the platforms at the intermediate stations was still in progress and not all the signals had been erected. Captain Coddington considered allowing the opening on 20 June, with a break of one mile around the Aln Viaduct, but felt that the track would be better consolidated and the Aln Viaduct completed if he deferred the opening until 1 July.[9] He thought the execution of the works was very good, and 'when complete will equal any railway in the country'. Unlike a modern jobsworth he did not insist on another inspection and trusted the railway company to finish the works to their established high standard.

Plate 4.2. A typical arch overbridge, No 73, north of Morpeth, which carried a farm road and public footpath. The clearance over the outer rails of just over 13 feet meant that the arch would have to be replaced prior to electrification. (BR)

Plate 4.3. (Below) The viaduct over the River Coquet (Bridge No 91), 30 miles north of Newcastle. Note the recessed arches in the piers; are these a decorative feature or were the piers originally pierced as on the High Level Bridge? (BR)

Plate 4.4. (Below left) Bothal Viaduct over the River Wansbeck (Bridge No 74), just north of Morpeth, has nine 50 feet spans and one of 12 feet. The recent concrete strengthening can be seen under the arches. (Bill Fawcett, 2009)

Plate 4.5. (Below right) The viaduct over the River Aln (Bridge No 110) with its 18 arches of 30 feet span. (Bill Fawcett)

The railway's impact was immediate as the last mail coach ran on the Great North Road just five days after it opened to Tweedmouth. Disappointingly, it was to be more than 15 months before Captain Simmons could approve the temporary viaduct over the Tweed allowing the first traffic to run from London to Edinburgh via the East-Coast.

The Royal Border Bridge

The North British Railway (NBR) from Edinburgh to the north bank of the Tweed had opened on 22 June 1846, but the contract for the N&B's bridge over the river was not let until 5 November 1846, and work was only sufficiently advanced to allow the foundation stone to be placed on 15 May 1847. The N&B had raised share capital well ahead of the expenditure on the contracts, so that was not a reason for the delayed start. Perhaps it was assumed that a simple masonry viaduct, even one of over 2,000 feet in length, would be a lot quicker to construct than the complex, double-deck, iron bridge over the Tyne with its long approach viaducts. If this was the case it did not work out, as the piles for the piers in the River Tweed were extremely difficult to drive. For example, the coffer dam and bearing piles for number 4 pier took 142 days to drive,[10] and the structure not was completed until a year after the High Level Bridge opened to rail traffic.

(Sir) George Barclay Bruce (1821-1908) was appointed the resident engineer to supervise the construction of the bridge, and he presented a paper about it to the Institution of Civil Engineers on 25 February 1851, which won him the Telford Medal.[11] His description of the site read: 'The ground where the railway crosses the river Tweed, is somewhat peculiar: the south side being a low plane gradually rising from the river, whereas on the north side, there is a steep bank, on top which stood the old castle of Berwick, celebrated more for its triumph of arms, than those of art.' He went on to explain that the south end of the viaduct was determined when the rising ground made the level of the rails of insufficient height for it to be continued economically. 'The semicircular arch was adopted as being the most elegant and imposing in so lofty a structure, and the span fixed upon that which best accorded with the height and length of the bridge.' The viaduct's compliance with its setting means it is now a Grade 1 listed structure. Railway historian, the late LTC Rolt, considered: 'Although there is nothing unique about it from an engineering point of view, there is no more romantic and evocative railway structure in the world than the Royal Border Bridge.'[12] (Colour Plate 5)

Bruce's paper did not make a single reference to Robert Stephenson, as designer of the bridge or his principal assistant TE Harrison. However, in the discussion following the paper, it was Stephenson who answered the questions on his choice of span and other design features. He had considered using large river spans and smaller ones over the land, but, in the end,

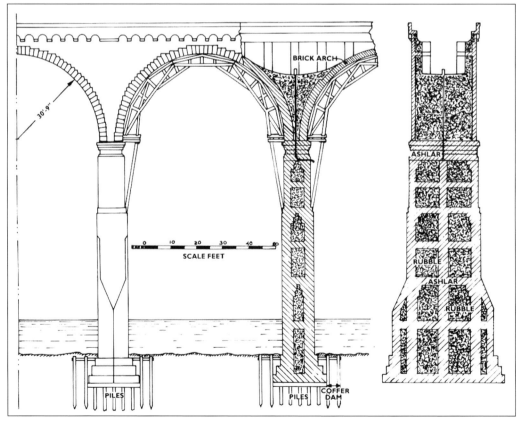

Figure 4.3. *Part elevation and section of the river spans for the Royal Border Bridge. The material under the river was gravel and sand which was considered sufficiently strong to support the piers, but the possibility of erosion during times of flooding suggested that piles extending as much as 40 feet to the bedrock should be used. Driving the piles through the gravel turned out to be very difficult and time consuming. The centres used to construct the arches were supported from the piers rather than from scaffolding at ground level, which could have been displaced by severe winter floods; this became a standard practice. (JFA)*

had standardized on piers at 70 feet centres throughout, giving 28 spans of 61 feet 6 inches. After the recent dramatic 'domino collapse' of Locke's Barentin Viaduct on the Paris-Rouen Railway, and two Yorkshire viaducts designed by other eminent engineers, he had decided to fill the voids within the ashlar piers with rubble to increase their stability. (Figure 4.3) At the mid point of the viaduct, on the south bank of the river, a much more substantial 'bastion pier' had been built as an additional precaution against problems arising during construction.

With the temporary viaduct over the Tyne having opened on 29 August 1848, giving a continuous railway from London to Tweedmouth, getting the trains across the Tweed became a top priority. The 14 arches south of the river were complete by 1848, but a timber staging, some 70 yards long and 25 feet high, was needed to join them to the almost finished embankment at their south end. Lack of suitable fill for this part of the embankment, and a slip in the material already placed required this temporary expedient.[13]

In order to provide a temporary viaduct over the river the first idea, as on the High Level Bridge, was to strengthen the contractors' scaffolding, being used to build the piers. This worked at both ends, but with the very slow progress of the pile driving, the piling engines still interfered with the erection of the scaffolding in the centre of the river. 'It was determined, consequently, to construct a separate wooden bridge [Figure 4.4], on the east side of the stone bridge. In order to make use of that part of the temporary bridge which had been previously erected, it was necessary to have two S curves.'[13] When Captain Simmons reported to the BOT on the temporary viaduct on 16 October 1848, he found it 'well and carefully put together, and upon sound principles', but he did recommend a 15 mph speed limit being imposed on the S curves, which were as sharp as 5 chains (100 metres).[14] Only seven weeks had elapsed from the trains first crossing the Tyne to the full service from London (Euston) to Edinburgh being introduced on 10 October; the first express trains took nearly 15 hours to complete their journey between the capitals.

The last arch of the bridge was keyed on 26 March 1850, and it was formally opened by Queen Victoria and Prince Albert on 29 August 1850. It had been intended to call the structure yet another 'Victoria Bridge' but 'Her Majesty was pleased to give it the name it now bears, "The Royal Border Bridge"'.

Other Bridges

There was a maximum of around 200 bridges between Newcastle and Berwick, but, despite a number of new roads crossing the south end of the line, the total is now less. The closure of many intermediate stations eliminated the need for their footbridges or subways, and changes of land ownership made some farm occupation bridges redundant. The need to raise most overbridges to provide electrification clearances meant that the elimination of little-used bridges could save a lot of money – Chathill, which remains open, even lost its footbridge. Most of the over bridges were masonry with a span of 30 feet, and a rise from the springing of the arch to its soffit of around 6 feet. (Plate 4.2) Unless they spanned deep cuttings their maximum clearance above the rails was insufficient for overhead electrification, and rebuilding them started in the late 1950s. (Plates 4.6 and 4.7)

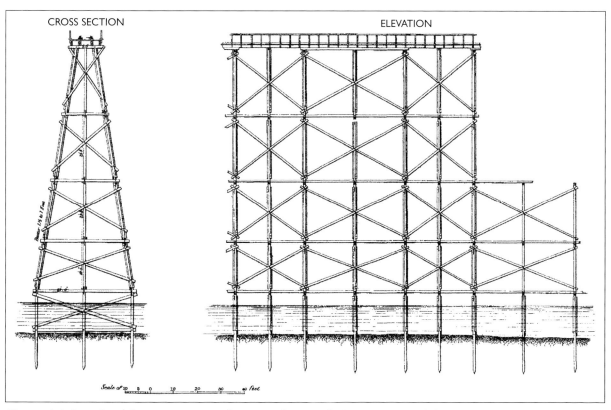

Figure 4.4. Details of the temporary viaduct over the Tweed. (Transactions of the Institution of Civil Engineers, 1851)

Plate 4.6. *The view north through Bridge No 158 (at Milepost 53½) on 28 October 1959. The bridge is in its as-built condition. (Note that the milepost was installed by the North Eastern Railway, not the Newcastle & Berwick.) (J⁰ Mallon / Joint NERA - Ken Hoole Study Centre Collection)*

Plate 4.7. Bridge No 150 carrying a minor road south of Belford, and to the same design as Bridge No 158, had its arch replaced by pre-cast concrete beams in 1962. The abutments, above the former springing of the arch, have been built up using pre-cast concrete blocks. As the carriageway level had to be raised by about 2 feet the wing walls have been heightened by two courses of almost matching stone, and the parapets have been carefully rebuilt. Later replacements sometimes used a method developed during the West-Coast electrification with pre-cast concrete arch rings being used instead of the beams. The well-maintained jointed-track is typical of the standards achieved on the Newcastle & Berwick at this time. (BR)

Endnotes:

1. For full account of the bridge see Addyman J and Fawcett W, *The High Level Bridge and Newcastle Central Station*, (1999) Chapter 4.

2. Captain Laffan's Report to BOT, 11 August 1849. National Archives MT6 7/101.

3. Jeaffreson JC and Pole W, *The Life of Robert Stephenson, Volume 2*, (1864) p 47.

4. Due to Hattersley's poor management they lost £39,435 on this contract. However, this should not be taken out of context as other contracts made their net profits, at this time, over £140,000. *Biographical Dictionary of Civil Engineers, Volume 2* (2008) p 583, also Nowell's journal in the Ken Hoole Study Centre, Darlington.

5. Its superstructure lasted until 1869 when it was replaced in wrought iron by TE Harrison.

6. Parris, H, *Government and Railways in Nineteenth-Century Britain,* (1965) pp 28-32.

7. Foster CB (Editor), *North Eastern Record, Volume 1,* (1988) p 42 Figure 2.6.

8. A large boggy area had to be crossed by the Liverpool & Manchester Railway at Chat Moss, and the method of dealing with it was largely followed in similar circumstances on other lines.

9. According to a gravestone in Tweedmouth churchyard (NT 996523) the first passenger train from Tweedmouth to Newcastle was driven by William Stephenson (1821-53).

10. *Proceedings of the Institution of Civil Engineers, Volume 10* (1851), pages 219-244. Bruce was the son of Dr John Bruce at whose academy Robert Stephenson had received his secondary education.

11. *Ibid.*

12. Rolt, LTC, *George and Robert Stephenson*, (1960) p 286.

13. *Proceedings of the Institution of Civil Engineers, Volume 10*, pp 229-30.

14. MT6 5/110.

Chapter 5 : The Buildings

Bill Fawcett

Introduction

The Newcastle & Berwick added to our stock of railway architecture in two significant ways: by sharing the cost of John Dobson and Robert Stephenson's magnificent Newcastle Central Station, and by providing a sequence of handsome 'Jacobethan' stations and goods sheds from the pen of Benjamin Green. Fortunately, much of this legacy survives, and we will begin by examining Dobson's contribution at Newcastle, excluding Central Station, which has been extensively covered in earlier books.[1]

John Dobson and the Railway at Manors

John Dobson (1787-1865) was the *doyen* of North-East architects when called on by George Hudson. He assisted with the land negotiations for the High Level Bridge and Newcastle Viaduct and designed two buildings for the sole use of the N&B: Manors passenger station and the Newcastle goods station, commonly known as Trafalgar Goods.

The origins of Manors station lie in the temporary terminus built by the Newcastle & North Shields Railway just west of their bridge over Trafalgar Street and opened in June 1839. This would be bypassed by the new line into Central Station but the North Shields line was a busy passenger route, carrying over half a million people in the first half of 1849, and Manors provided good access to much of the town centre. Hudson therefore agreed to provide a replacement alongside, and Dobson's plans were approved by what had become the York, Newcastle & Berwick Railway in April 1849, only weeks before Hudson's resignation.[2] (Figure 5.1)

The new Manors station comprised a pair of platforms set high above the street, with a single building, situated on the eastbound side, which would be the departure platform for most passengers. The station office was a small but powerful looking structure, built of sandstone ashlar in a somewhat Italianate manner, with a sequence of arched openings framed by boldly rusticated piers. (Figure 5.2)

Traffic continued to grow, and the North Eastern Railway carried out a series of enlargements at Manors which finally resulted in one of their most interesting medium-scale stations. The first stage came in 1872-3, with a considerable lengthening of the platforms, which were given extensive roofs, virtually hiding the original building.[3] Meanwhile, congestion was building up on the route itself, and only a dozen years later the NER embarked on widening the route from two tracks to four between Manors and Heaton Junction. This entailed widening the Manors site to the south, where the land falls away towards the Tyne, so that the enlarged station, designed by the NER architect William Bell, presented a three-storey frontage on that side, with the waiting rooms on the top floor and shops at the bottom. (Figure 5.3)

The work of widening the line, enlarging Manors and building a new station at Heaton was placed in the capable hands of the Tyneside contractor Walter Scott and began in 1885.[4] It entailed replacing the old westbound platform (No 2) by an island (Nos 2 & 3) and building a fourth platform. The building and awning on Platform 1 were unaltered but the new platforms were given spacious ridge and furrow roofs with elaborate and handsome ironwork. Pedestrian access was by a subway from which a flight of steps led down to the street on the south side. (Plate 5.1)

The final enlargement was prompted by the need to link up with the Newcastle branch of the Blyth & Tyne Railway, which merged into the NER during 1874. This had its own terminus at New Bridge Street, only a few hundred yards north of Manors, but the NER was reluctant to extend the line down to Manors because of the considerable costs involved.

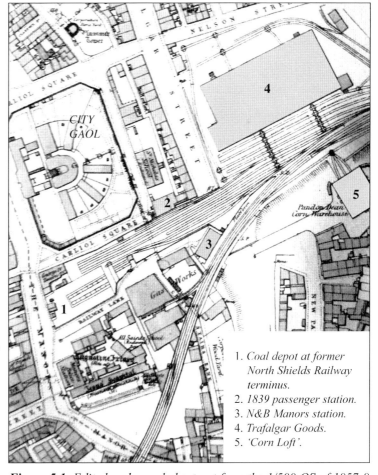

1. *Coal depot at former North Shields Railway terminus.*
2. *1839 passenger station.*
3. *N&B Manors station.*
4. *Trafalgar Goods.*
5. *'Corn Loft'.*

Figure 5.1. *Edited and rescaled extract from the 1/500 OS of 1857-8 (north at the top). This shows the N&B approaching on the viaduct from Central Station and passing through Manors station (3) before reaching the junction with the tracks into the old Carliol Square terminus.*

Eventually they bowed to local pressure, and the new line opened on 1 January 1909. To make the junction, it was necessary to demolish the original Manors station building which was replaced by one facing Trafalgar Street. Designed again by William Bell and his staff, this featured a hip-roofed booking hall, detailed in washable terracotta and faience, and crowned by a stylish clock cupola. (Plate 5.2) Serving the new line were two through platforms and three bays, which were designated Manors North, while the existing station was referred to as Manors East.

The most striking feature of Manors North was its enormous array of fully-glazed platform roofing, probably designed by Bell's structural specialist Robert Parkin. The use of steel sections (instead of wrought iron) and trussed beams made for a much lighter and more elegant structure than that of the 1885 Manors East roof, and this was coupled with a more restrained approach to detailing. All this has gone, and all that remains today is a bare island platform serving the occasional stopping train on the Berwick line. Most of Manors station was made redundant by the construction of the Tyne & Wear Metro in the nineteen-seventies, and the diversion of suburban traffic into tunnels beneath the city centre. Some of the Manors North roofing and features from its booking hall were salvaged for re-use elsewhere, notably at the *Marsden Rattler* public house on the sea-front in South Shields.

Dobson's other contribution to the railway scene at Manors was the Trafalgar goods station, built on the north side of the line just east of the junction with the route into the original North Shields Railway terminus, which was retained as a coal depot. Trafalgar goods was roofed in five spans, ranged behind a series of sidings from which wagon turntables gave access to tracks running through spans 2 and 4. Each track would have served a transhipment platform with a cart road on the other side, one platform being allocated to received goods and the other to outward traffic. (Plate 5.3)

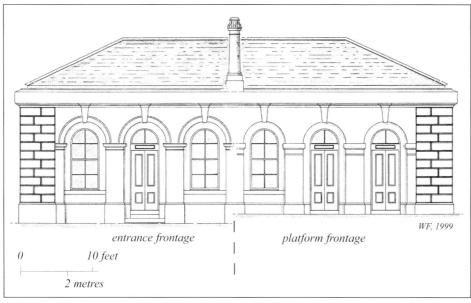

entrance frontage   platform frontage

WF, 1999

0   10 feet

2 metres

Figure 5.2. Front and rear elevations of John Dobson's 1850 Manors station. (*Bill Fawcett*)

Figure 5.3. Manors station at its maximum extent in 1909, after completion of the link to New Bridge Street. (*Bill Fawcett*)

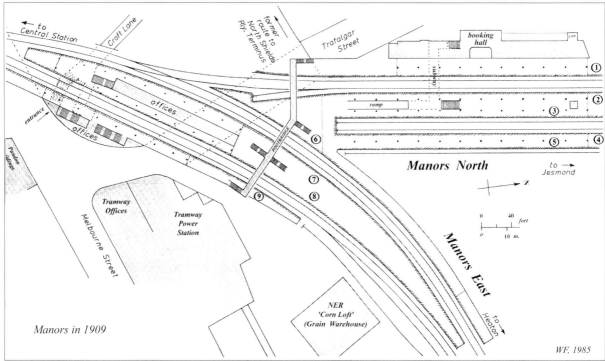

Manors in 1909

Goods handling was assisted by the provision of hydraulic cranes, a recent innovation by another Tyneside entrepreneur, William (later Lord) Armstrong.

The building was constructed on made-up ground, town rubbish having been used for some years to fill in the steep-sided valley of the culverted Pandon Burn. On this unpromising material, 'for the most part in a state of fermentation'[5], Dobson spread the load by employing extended concrete footings, varying in width from six to fourteen feet. Outwardly, this was one of the most monumentally stylish of goods stations, with the individual roof bays expressed as pedimented gables separated by pairs of boldly-rusticated pilaster strips.

For two decades Trafalgar was the principal NER goods station in Newcastle, until the opening of the enormous Forth Goods in two stages in 1871 and 1874. Trafalgar remained busy, however, but fell victim to the Blyth & Tyne link. A replacement was provided on the north side of New Bridge Street, a tall reinforced concrete building incorporating a grain store.[6] This was designed in 1903 and its completion allowed the demolition of Trafalgar Goods, with Manors North station being built on its site.

Plate 5.1. View along Platform 8, looking towards Central Station, with the 1880s island platform and its distinctive ridge-and-furrow roofing to the right of the Class 37-hauled permanent way train. (John M Fleming, 1973)

Plate 5.2. The entrance to Manors station seen from Trafalgar Street in the 1960s, with the prominent cupola surmounting the booking hall. (Bill Fawcett)

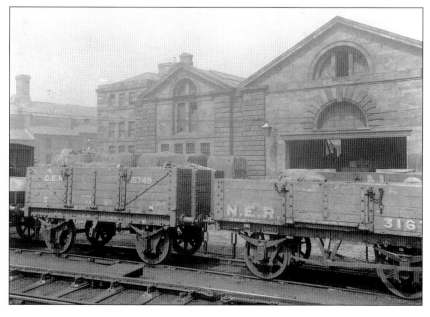

Plate 5.3. Trafalgar Goods Station in the early 1900s, looking northwest. The NER has formed the large opening to make for easier access. (Tony Cormack Collection)

Benjamin Green

Brand images were invented by the Victorians, and Benjamin Green's succession of stylish stations is, even today, an important element in defining the visual identity of the Newcastle & Berwick route. He enjoyed a good start in life, his father being John Green (1787-1852), architect and bridge designer, who's most notable works are the innovative timber viaducts which he designed for the Newcastle & North Shields Railway.[7]

Benjamin Green (1813-1858) will have learned the basics from his father before going to London to polish his art at the hands of Auguste Pugin, father of the great Gothic designer and polemicist Augustus Welby Pugin. Benjamin then became his father's partner and collaborated with him on the work for the Newcastle & North Shields Railway, including the North Shields terminus, which featured an innovative arched timber trainshed and an office building spanning the tracks. The latter was Tudor in style, with mullioned windows and steep gables crowned by ball finials. This is close to the forms Benjamin would use on the Berwick line,

but a further step towards those is provided by the terminus provided for the extension of the North Shields line to Tynemouth.[8] In this the hoodmouldings, which run round the top of the North Shields windows, are dispensed with to give a more crisply elegant appearance, inspired by late Elizabethan and Jacobean designs, hence the common usage of the term 'Jacobethan'. The style had been popularized in country house work by architects such as William Burn, and retained a suavely manorial feel when employed by Green on the Berwick railway.

By the time the contract was let for Tynemouth, in March 1846, Hudson was about to take over the North Shields Railway and was already well acquainted with the Greens, having originally adopted their plan for a high level road bridge across the Tyne at Newcastle. It was, therefore, a short step and perhaps even a consolation prize to offer them the design of most of the N&B buildings. Benjamin went on to design all the original buildings between Heaton Junction and Tweedmouth, together with those on the Kelso and Alnwick branches and the 'corn loft' at Manors.

Plate 5.4. Acklington station in 1973, almost in its original condition, complete with Benjamin Green's distinctive platform verandahs. The LNER nameboard, with its cut-out letters, had survived 25 years of nationalisation. (Bill Fawcett)

Figure 5.4. Acklington station; edited version of NER floor plans showing how the two dwellings and the passenger accommodation were interleaved with each other. (Bill Fawcett)

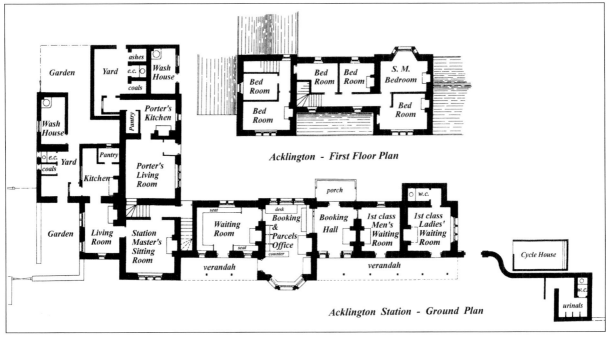

Acklington - First Floor Plan

Acklington Station - Ground Plan

Stations

Most of the original stations were variants on two designs, exemplified by Acklington and Chathill, which both survive and which show the most ambitious form, in which a porter's dwelling is incorporated with the station house and offices to justify a larger building than would otherwise be required. This is then given a picturesque L-plan layout, framing the station forecourt. All were constructed from one of Britain's finest building stones, the Northumbrian freestone. This is a fine-grained but durable sandstone which is easily worked to the smooth ashlar finish and crisp mouldings which Green desired.

Acklington represents the most common design, with a platform frontage comprising a pair of gables clasping between them a distinctive platform verandah, carried on square cast-iron posts and fretted brackets. (Plate 5.4) The stationmaster's house occupied the ground floor of the left gable and the upper floor of the whole platform range, with the porter's house in the wing stretching behind. Despite the imposing appearance overall, the station facilities appear to have been confined originally to just three rooms on the ground floor: entrance hall, office and waiting room, with the public entrance through a handsome, tripartite, composition door flanked by windows – on the road side of the right-hand wing.

Additional accommodation was provided by the NER who built out the low wing to the right, scrupulously conforming, as usual, to the original style – the only difference is the slightly Gothic stepping of the lower part of the NER chimney stacks. This extra space enabled them to provide separate First Class waiting rooms for men and women and to resite the entrance/booking hall. The office could then be extended into the former entrance hall to provide more space for handling the important parcels business. Comparable extensions were made at many other stations. (Figure 5.4)

Versions of the Acklington pattern were provided at Killingworth, Morpeth, Warkworth, Longhoughton, Christon Bank and Belford, though only Warkworth includes the secondary range for the porter's house. Warkworth is a very picturesque affair with the railway some feet above ground level and the station therefore built on a prominent basement and approached by a broad flight of steps leading to an arched portico of the sort already used at Tynemouth, tucked into one gable. (Plate 5.5) The porter's wing has its ground floor at the level of the station basement and thus forms a very effective visual buttress to the composition.

Longhoughton also saw the railway running well above ground level, but the solution adopted was less

satisfactory. (Plate 5.6) The two-storey building had the platforms and offices at first-floor level, reached by a flight of external steps, with some of the living accommodation backing on to the railway embankment. Morpeth repeats the portico treatment found at Warkworth, and also Belford, and is the only one of Green's stations to remain in railway use for office and waiting rooms; the other surviving ones have all become private houses. NER extensions to Morpeth are dealt with in Chapter 6.

Plate 5.5. *The grand entrance to Warkworth station, showing the gothic portico, tucked into the gable, which was a feature of many of these stations, such as Morpeth and Belford. (Colin B Foster)*

Plate 5.6. *Longhoughton station, with the platforms at the upper level and the diminutive goods shed just visible on the left. Most of the domestic accommodation was on the ground floor, backing on to the railway embankment. (John F Mallon)*

Chathill displays an alternative approach, with a central gable on the platform frontage, flanked by verandahs. (Plate 5.7) The centrepiece features a canted bay window, which rises through two storeys and is then corbelled out to become the gable. The same idea was employed at Stannington (Plate 5.8) but at Lucker it was extended to finish in a pair of gabled cross-wings, effectively a synthesis of the two main types. Lucker owed this *largesse* to the covenant which Hudson made with the Duke of Northumberland on 26 April 1845.[9] This stipulated that Lucker, which served the coastal townships of Bamburgh and North Sunderland, should be a 'first-class' station along with Warkworth, a ducal domain, and the station at the Alnwick Branch junction. Green produced an interesting variant at Longhirst and Beal (Plate 5.9), each of which comprised a pair of houses, formally presented as distinct two-storey blocks linked by a one-storey office range fronted by a verandah.

One step down from all these buildings are the stations at Scremerston and Widdrington. (Plates 5.10 and 5.11) These forsake the stern gables of the larger stations in favour of overhanging roofs with finialled bargeboards; otherwise their vocabulary is the same but the effect is more informal. Slightly smaller than these, but more formal in appearance with a fine display of ball finials, were the private stations at Fallodon (Plate 5.12) and Little Mill. Fallodon was built for Sir George Grey, who became Home Secretary in Lord John Russell's 1847 cabinet. His grandson, Sir Edward Grey, served as NER chairman prior to his appointment as Foreign Secretary at the end of 1905 so Fallodon saw plenty of distinguished visitors. As Viscount Grey, he resumed his railway career as a director of the LNER but died in 1933, after which the station was closed by agreement with the new owner of the Fallodon estate.[10]

Plate 5.7. Chathill station in 1973. The room on the left, with the bay window, is an extra waiting room added by the NER in a sympathetic style. The station originally had a verandah to the right of the central canted bay, but that had long been lost. (Bill Fawcett)

Plate 5.8. Stannington, seen in NER days, had recently lost its verandah on the right-hand side. (Lens of Sutton Association)

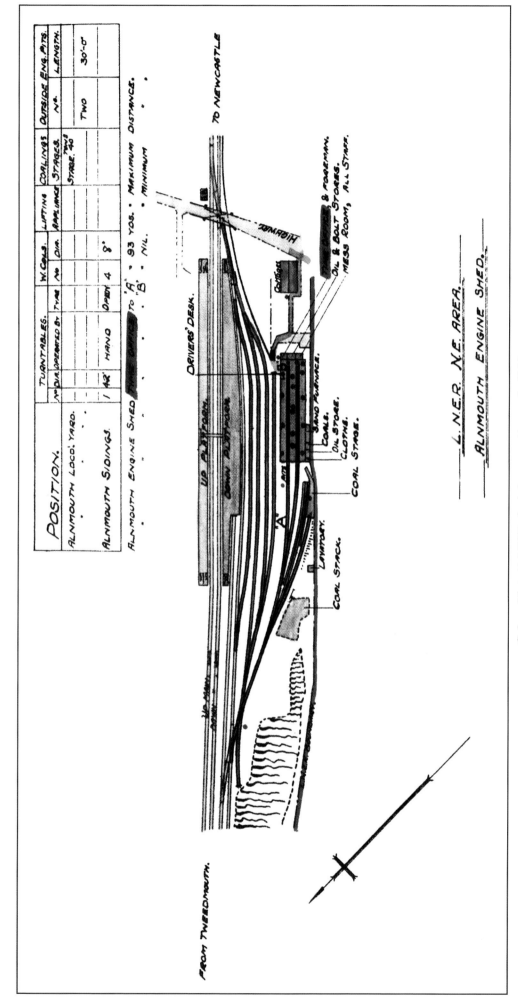

Colour Plate 7. LNER shed diagram, Alnmouth, 1929.

39

Velvet Hall Station.

Colour Plate 8. *Velvet Hall station, on the N&BR's Kelso Branch. The view is looking towards Tweedmouth, and was taken before building of the 1905 extension to the station house. (JC Dean Collection)*

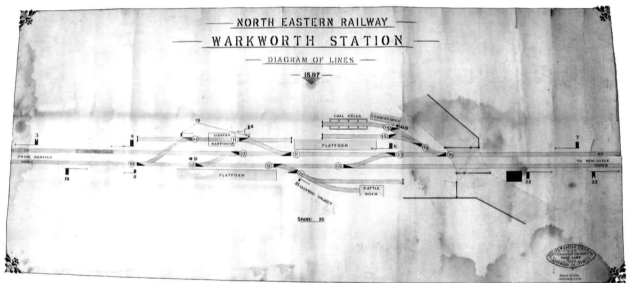

Colour Plate 9. *Warkworth signal cabin diagram, produced by the Permanent Way Department at Park Lane, Gateshead, when a new cabin was provided in 1897. Home and starting signals are provided in each direction and a track circuit has been added subsequently in rear of the Up Home (No 4). However, not all moves are covered by fixed signals – such as backing from the Up Main to the coal cells would have been hand-signalled from the cabin. (Original diagram from the CJ Woolstenholmes Collection; seen here modestly digitally restored, but still showing its age.)*

Colour Plate 10. *The third signal cabin at Belford was to a new design and was commissioned in early 1962; the inclined windows and roof overhang were intended to reduce glare. The cabin, seen here on 2 June 1963, is directly opposite the second (bridge) cabin, which was subsequently demolished. The relay room is lit by roof lights, and a North Eastern Region tangerine name board adds a dash of colour to the otherwise subdued tones. Boom gates would replace the electrically-worked conventional gates in September 1966. Belford would close after 28 years' service; although the relay room remains in use, the upper floor has been removed. (John M Boyes / Armstrong Railway Photographic Trust)*

Plate 5.9. Beal station: the nearer of the two houses was that of the stationmaster and his family, linked by the one-storey office range to the porter's house at the far end. (JC Dean, 1964)

Plate 5.10. Scremerston, looking towards Berwick, photographed by JC Dean in 1973. The building retains an impressive array of finials hanging from the bargeboards.

Plate 5.11. Widdrington station, with an unsympathetic treatment of the bay window. (JC Dean, 1967)

Plate 5.12. *Fallodon station circa 1930.* (*Henry Wilson Books*)

Plate 5.13. *Forest Hall's modest but dignified building with a leg of the elevated signalbox on the right.* (*John M Fleming, 1963*)

Little Mill served Earl Grey's Howick Estate and became a public station in 1861, its regular services augmented by a right to stop trains which was only rescinded following the death of the fourth Earl Grey, an NER director, in 1917.

At the bottom of the pecking order is a group of station houses which are almost as big as the two private ones but got a distinctly plainer treatment. These comprise Forest Hall, Plessey, the short-lived Lesbury station, Smeafield and Goswick. Of these, only Lesbury (Chapter 6) originated as a passenger station; Forest Hall (Plate 5.13) became one in 1856, Plessey in 1859, Smeafield in 1871 and Goswick in 1870 (masquerading under the name Windmill Hill until the start of 1898). The same design was also used for a crossing house at Ulgham Grange which never became a station. Given that these houses are much larger than a standard crossing cottage, it is tempting to speculate that they may have been provided at locations where some sort of goods traffic was handled at the outset.

A distinctive feature of N&B stations was Benjamin Green's standard waiting shed, provided on the opposite platform to each of his station houses. It follows a convention of the time in being a pent roof (monopitch) structure but, unusually, the roof slopes down from the rear wall towards the platform frontage. The sheds were originally open fronted, employing the same columns and brackets as seen in the station verandahs, but the NER gradually closed in the fronts, usually with a band of windows above a planked dado, and even pandered to passenger comfort to the extent of introducing heating stoves. (Plate 5.14)

One station stood out from all the others, and this was Tweedmouth, equipped with a trainshed and employing a more expensive version of the Jacobethan repertoire, with shaped gables and an arcaded portico. This is considered further in Chapter 6.

Crossing Cottages and Other Housing

The standard crossing cottage was a much more modest affair than the houses seen at places like Goswick. The picturesque one-storey and attic design comprised a pair of houses, with the front roof swept down over a pair of mullioned, rectangular bay windows with the doorways inset between them. The accommodation provided was much less than in the crossing houses being built for Hudson's Yorkshire lines at the same time by his friend George Townsend Andrews, indicating the degree of freedom allowed to each architect and, perhaps, the humble expectations of Northumbrian countryfolk. (Plate 5.15)

Newham crossing became a station in 1851 but did not acquire anything substantial in the way of buildings, though the NER did provide a wooden waiting-room block. Chevington (Plate 5.16) became a station in 1870 and was given some wooden offices, while in 1898-9 the NER added a spacious new stationmaster's house, built to a standard design of its then architect, William Bell, and set well back from the railway.

In general, railway housing was confined to the stations and crossing houses, the latter sometimes being occupied by a platelayer whose family took charge of the gates. An exception was made at Tweedmouth, where housing was provided for enginemen in the form of a neat terrace with Jacobethan detailing to comply with the nearby station.

Plate 5.14. Acklington, seen here above, and Chathill are the two locations which retain Green's original waiting sheds, providing shelter on the opposite platform from the main buildings. Originally, it was open-fronted but the waist-high boarding and windows were provided by the NER. (Bill Fawcett, 1973)

Plate 5.15. Ulgham Lane crossing, with one of Green's standard cottage pairs. (JC Dean, 1967)

Plate 5.16. Preparing to cut a rail at Chevington station. The original cottages are seen to the right of the level crossing, with later timber offices provided by the NER. Note the staggered platforms. (John F Mallon Collection)

43

Goods Sheds

To deck out passenger stations in a picturesque fashion was common practice in the eighteen-forties, albeit that the Berwick line ones were uncommonly well done. It was unusual to extend this treatment to less public buildings such as goods and engine sheds, yet Green applied his Jacobethan treatment to these as well. An exception was the 'corn loft', or grain warehouse, built to the east of Manors station. This was designed by Green in an Italianate style to fit in with Dobson's station, with vertical strips of windows and loading doors arched at the top floor and framed by rusticated pilaster strips. Although it was a five-storey building, the fall of the land placed the top floor at rail level. It was superseded as a grain store by the ferroconcrete New Bridge Street warehouse and was housing other combustible foodstuffs when hit by a bomb during the Second World War. The building evidently burned for days and was never reinstated, but the complete shell survived into the nineteen-sixties. (Plate 5.17)

Fortunately, two of Green's country goods sheds survive to demonstrate the application of Jacobethan forms; these are Acklington (Plate 5.18) and Christon Bank. Acklington is a particularly well-proportioned building and is based on a plan form which had evolved during the eighteen-forties. A railway track ran the length of the building, flanked by a wooden platform into which a cart dock was set from the opposite side, the platform was equipped with a hand crane, swivelling round on a vertical post fixed between the deck and roof structure. Built on to the south gable was a small stable, in matching style. Similar goods sheds, in a variety of sizes, were provided at other stations, with features to suit the locality, as at Longhoughton (Plate 9.15) where the shed was actually aligned at right angles to the running lines. The largest were at Belford (Plate 5.19) and Tweedmouth, which had three cart bays and was later converted into a repair shop for the nearby engine shed.

The Branches

By the summer of 1848 the state of the national economy meant that even Hudson was having to rein in his ambitions. On the N&B there was little scope for savings in capital expenditure other than in those buildings which were still outstanding, namely those on the Kelso and Alnwick branches and Central Station, which had to do without its portico for a further dozen years.

Contracts for the Kelso Branch buildings were let on 27 January 1849.[11] The stations were smaller and simpler than the general run of those on the main line but they were not without grace, having neat mullioned windows and shapely chimneys (see Chapter 7).

The Alnwick Branch was a much sorrier story.

Tenders for its buildings were invited in June 1850, by which time Hudson was in disgrace although his old cronies were still running the YN&B Board.[12] They, however, were under strong pressure to demonstrate that economies were being made and the station offices at Alnwick and Bilton Junction (later renamed Alnmouth) made the point. Though designed by Green, they were small, plain and undistinguished – in happier times they might just have passed for a railway stable. The station houses were separate buildings of rather more grace, featuring stately gabled doorcases. This almost marked the end of Benjamin Green's short but distinguished career as a railway architect. His final work in that field was for the Alston Branch of the Newcastle & Carlisle Railway.

Plate 5.17. *The Manors 'corn loft' seen in the 1960s, not long before demolition. Unusually for Green, it is not Jacobethan but is designed to harmonise with Dobson's Manors station. (John M Fleming)*

Alnwick was particularly galling since Hudson and Green must originally have had in mind something like Tweedmouth to serve the ducal seat. Yet in the long term the miserable nature of the original station proved a blessing since it shamed the NER into providing a splendid new one in connection with the opening of the Alnwick & Cornhill line in 1887. The outcome was the finest branch-line terminus produced by William Bell during his long years as NER Architect, featuring a trainshed which, from the tracks, looks like a scaled-down version of its main-line contemporary at Darlington Bank Top.

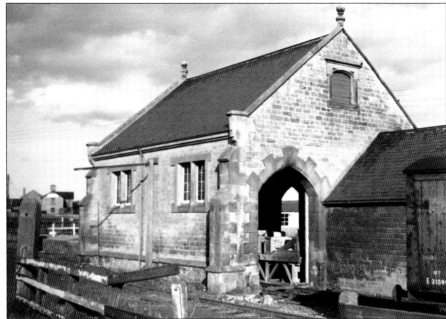

Plate 5.18. Acklington goods shed, which survives converted into a dwelling. (John M Fleming, 1966)

Plate 5.19. Except for Trafalgar Goods, Belford was the largest of the N&B's goods sheds. It was strategically placed to be the railhead for a large area extending from the coast to Wooler and Glendale. Class K1 No 62024 is seen on the pick-up goods on 14 July 1966, barely seven months before its withdrawal. (John M Fleming)

Later Stations

Cramlington (Plate 5.20) is something of an oddity. It was one of the original stations, equipped with a standard waiting shed on the Down platform, yet the Up platform boasted nothing more than a temporary timber office. The situation was remedied in the early months of 1854, by which time the YN&B was working in partnership with the two companies with which it would merge later that year to form the North Eastern Railway.[13] As a result, the job of designing the station building was given to Thomas Cabry, the engineer of the York & North Midland Railway. Cabry's solution was a neat, low, hip-roofed brick office range with the centre recessed to provide a sheltered waiting area. It was very different from the N&B house style but infinitely better than Alnwick or Bilton.

The NER had little need to add to the station stock of the Newcastle & Berwick. Most change was seen at Morpeth and Alnmouth, which are dealt with in Chapter 6. Otherwise it was largely a matter of minor extensions, done in keeping with the original style. Two wholly new stations were built, however: Annitsford (Plate 5.21) and Pegswood. Annitsford originated in 1860 as a station serving the mining settlement of Dudley Colliery, which was the name it originally bore but which was changed to Dudley in 1874. The original accommodation was no doubt minimal but in 1877 a substantial station was built on a new site, being renamed Annitsford shortly after completion.[14] It was designed during the short period when William Peachey was NER Architect and bore all the hallmarks of his style. The platform was at first-floor level, where it was an H-plan building with the wings framing a spacious waiting area fronted by a glazed screen.

Pegswood (Plate 5.22), situated between Morpeth and Longhirst, was another response to the growth of mining communities in south-east Northumberland. The decision to provide a station there was taken in August 1899, with the contract being let early in 1902, and it opened at the start of 1903.[15] The platforms were given neat but undistinguished brick waiting rooms reached by ramps leading down from a road bridge at the north end. William Bell's design also provided for a small overtrack booking office adjacent to the bridge. Though the station remains open, the buildings have gone but the typical Bell stationmaster's house, set some way back to the east, remains.

An enigma is posed by the crossing house at Crag Mill (Plate 5.23), which enjoyed a brief career as a station in the eighteen-seventies.[16] Crag Mill lies less than a mile north of Belford station on a minor road leading from Belford to Waren Mill and thence Bamburgh. The house is built in brick, to a totally different design from the other N&B buildings, although the proportions and the use of stone-capped raking parapets mean that it does not look out of place. Perhaps it is an early work by the first NER Architect, Thomas Prosser.

Costs, Contractors and Carnage

In 1849 Benjamin Green was asked to submit a detailed account of the expenditure on buildings. The resulting volume survives and gives a very interesting picture of how the costs were made up.[17] It is inappropriate to go into full detail here, but a few examples should give the picture. Many of the buildings were constructed by the contractors for the line, thus McKay and Blackstock did all of those at Tweedmouth along with Christon Bank, Fallodon, Chathill, Lucker and Belford. However, the plasterwork throughout was let to Ralph Dodds, the distinguished Newcastle plasterer who was also engaged on Central Station. The ironwork for the station and engine-shed roofs at Tweedmouth was supplied and erected by Hawks Crawshay, then engaged on the High Level Bridge. The masonry contractors for the bridge and the Newcastle Viaduct,

Plate 5.20. Cramlington station captured by JC Dean in the 1960s. The goods shed, behind the footbridge, was designed by Cabry at the same time as the station. The Green waiting shed, just visible on the right, dated from the opening of the line. View looking south through the road bridge which had been rebuilt to electrification clearances as early as 1961, 30 years before electrification came about.

Plate 5.21. Annitsford station. (Lens of Sutton Association)

Rush & Lawton, were also building the Killingworth section of the line and got the contract for the Trafalgar goods station. They did not, however, win the contract for the buildings on the Killingworth section. The masonry work for Killingworth, Stannington (named Netherton until 1892) and Longhirst went to James Dunlop with other tradesmen contracting separately for tasks such as carpentry and slating.

Green's account for Killingworth provides a good picture of how the costs were made up. The first payment was made on 26 November 1846 and the last on 27 February 1849, with the total expenditure coming to £2,562-6-11. This was made up of:

station building	1,128-18-9
waiting shed	158-0-1
platforms	639-6-3
coal depots	222-17-3
yard office and weighbridge	122-18-7
walls and gates	80-5-9
fittings (lamps *etc.*)	87-10-0
well and pumps	30-12-2
metalling roadway	88-17-0

The well is a reminder that most stations, situated in rural areas, had to be totally self-sufficient.

The figure for the station building is typical. Acklington cost £1,085, Longhoughton £1,101 and Chathill £1,119. However, the disjointed houses at Longhirst and Beal came in at £1,281 and £1,454, while Warkworth was £1,649 and Tweedmouth came in at a princely £8,629. Scremerston and Widdrington displayed some saving, with the buildings costing £918 and £739. The private stations at Fallodon and Little Mill cost £696 and £741 for buildings and £868 and £1,288 in total, the higher cost of the latter reflecting the provision of some depot facilities. At the bottom of the scale, Lesbury cost £402-11-9.

Plate 5.22. Pegswood station, showing the modest timber overtrack booking office at the north end, adjacent to the original road bridge. (Lens of Sutton Association)

Plate 5.23. Crag Mill. Like many of the N&B crossings it still retained manual control long after the Heaton - Burnmouth resignalling of 1962. (John M Fleming, 1966)

Acklington goods shed, which survives, cost £688-16-0 but this is towards the bottom end of the range, Longhoughton being the cheapest, at £428. The highest price was the £2,251 paid for Belford, railhead for some of the coastal townships. This was actually more expensive than Tweedmouth. A typical pair of gate cottages, Dam Dykes, cost £530-10-8.

Busy main lines are not conducive to the survival of early buildings. Thus only one original station survives between York and Darlington. Fortunately, the traffic thins out north of Newcastle; there has not been the same need for line widening, and a majority of Benjamin Green's elegant works survive. Heading north from Heaton Junction, the survivors are Stannington, Morpeth, Longhirst, Widdrington, Acklington, Warkworth, Lesbury, Christon Bank, Chathill, Belford, Smeafield, Goswick and Scremerston. Acklington and Chathill are particularly appealing since both stations remain open and retain their waiting sheds. Acklington and Christon Bank also retain their goods sheds, both converted into houses.

Again heading north from Heaton, the losses are Forest Hall, Killingworth, Cramlington, Plessey, Alnmouth, Longhoughton, Little Mill, Fallodon, Lucker and Beal. (Plate 5.24) Tweedmouth is a bleak picture: all the N&B buildings have gone and the NER engine shed (a square 'roundhouse' of 1878) clings tenuously to life, having lost part of its roof. The NER buildings at Annitsford and Pegswood have vanished but NER housing survives at a variety of locations. The only serious loss on the Kelso Branch has been Cornhill station, while Alnwick continues to make a fine impression in its modern role as the home to Barter Books.

Endnotes:

1. John F Addyman & Bill Fawcett, *The High Level Bridge & Newcastle Central Station,* NERA for the 150th Anniversary Committee, (1999). Bill Fawcett, *A History of North Eastern Railway Architecture Volume 1*, NERA, (2001).
2. YN&B Board 10 & 16 April 1849 (National Archives RAIL 772/3).
3. NER Locomotive & Works Committee 9 February, 31 May, 13 December 1872 (National Archives RAIL 527/30). For more detail and drawings see Bill Fawcett, *A History of North Eastern Railway Architecture Volume 3,* NERA, (2005).
4. Way & Works Committee 1 October 1885 (National Archives RAIL 527/38).
5. Address by Dobson to the Northern Architectural Association on 19 April 1859, reproduced in full in Lyall Wilkes, *John Dobson*, Oriel Press, (1980). A more reliable source than Wilkes for Dobson's career is Thomas Faulkner & Andrew Greg, *John Dobson*, Tyne Bridge Publishing, (2001).
6. Designed by the NER's William Bell in association with the consultant LG Mouchel, it represented an early application of the Hennebique ferroconcrete system to railway warehouses. The upper floors were destroyed in the Second World War and the remainder in the 1970s. Illustrations appear in Bill Fawcett, *op. cit.* note 3.
7. The Ouseburn Viaduct, which still carries the main line, was reconstructed in wrought iron in 1869 and widened to four tracks in 1885. Biographical details of the Greens are given in Bill Fawcett, *op. cit.* note 1. Their entry in Howard Colvin's admirable *Biographical Dictionary of British Architects* unfortunately confuses some of the works of John Green and his nephew John Green Junior.
8. The building survives in Oxford Road, Tynemouth, though the platforms and accompanying hotel have gone.
9. See also Chapter 2.
10. Hudson made a formal agreement with Sir George Grey on 22 January 1846. The LNER Traffic Committee, 15 February 1934, gave the new Fallodon owner Captain Graves and his wife free First Class *All Station Passes* for life in return for giving up the station.
11. YN&B Board 22 January 1849 considered tenders and on the 27th Hudson and Green met the contractors to negotiate a price and let the contract, as reported to the Board on 13 February (National Archives RAIL 772/3).
12. *Newcastle Journal*, 15 June 1850.
13. Joint Locomotive & Stores Committee of the YN&B, Y&NM and Leeds Northern Railways 2 September and 9 December 1853 (National Archives RAIL 527/23).
14. NER Locomotive Committee 14 September 1876 asked Peachey to submit a plan as soon as possible. 1 February let the contract but a fortnight later it was re-let to Douglas & Wilson for £2,503-3-10 (National Archives RAIL 527/32).
15. NER Way & Works Committee 30 January 1902 (National Archives RAIL 527/46).
16. Crag Mill was open from February 1871 to October 1877 according to Alan Young (see Appendix 1), which has been used to check other station dates.
17. National Archives RAIL 772/52.

Plate 5.24. *A poignant view of the last days of the once-splendid Lucker station. (Ken Hoole Study Centre)*

Chapter 6 : Morpeth, Alnmouth and Tweedmouth

John F Addyman and Bill Fawcett

Morpeth

Today's railway users at Morpeth should be grateful to Earl Grey; had the original 1839 GNBR alignment, with its branch line to the town (Figure 6.1), been allowed to proceed it would, like Alnwick, almost certainly have lost its rail link in the 1960s. Morpeth station is situated at the east end of the 90 degrees, 20 chains (400 metre) curve that was forced upon the N&B to get the main line as near to the town as possible to gain its support in preference to the Brunel scheme. The curve, which was restricted to 40 mph, has been the scene of high-speed derailments in 1969 and 1984; both were due to driver's errors. These could have been avoided if, following the introduction of the 1955 British Railways Modernisation Plan, Morpeth curve had been given a major realignment, which would have bypassed the station, and probably also have led to its closure. However, housing developments had already blocked the obvious line south from the Wansbeck Viaduct.[1]

Morpeth, being completed before the economies following Hudson's downfall, had elegant station buildings and reasonable facilities from the outset, but, unlike Tweedmouth, it did not get a trainshed. The costs given in the architects, John and Benjamin Green's, account book include: main station buildings on up platform £2,632; platforms and boundary walls £800; waiting shed on Down platform £251; goods warehouse £1,809; coal depot £1,228; two offices and weighbridges £263; cattle docks £220; stables £77; road and steps to station £246. These plus sundry items, including a turntable and water cranes, made the total cost nearly £9,500.[2] Railway politics initially prevented Morpeth from becoming the junction station for two branch passenger services that reached the town in 1858 and 1862. (Figure 6.2) The differences were resolved in the 1870s, and major changes were made by 1880 allowing both services to use the NER station; extensive awnings were erected over all the platforms in 1890-1. Plate 6.1 shows almost the full extent of the station's development.

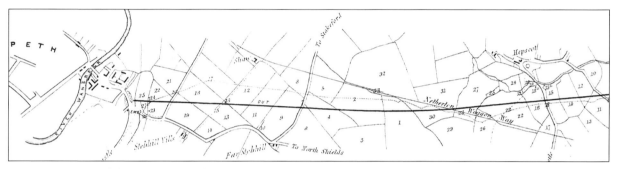

Figure 6.1. *Part of the GNBR 1839 deposited plan showing the line of its proposed branch into Morpeth.*

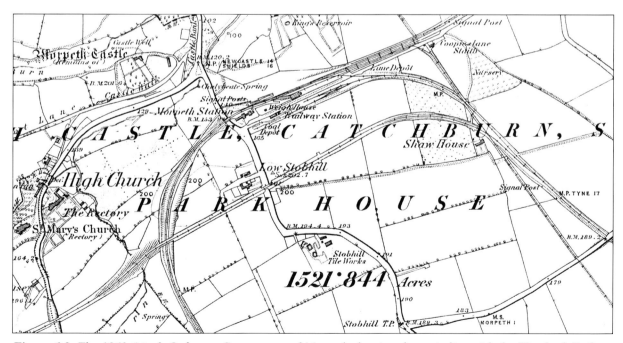

Figure 6.2. *The 1863 6 inch Ordnance Survey map of Morpeth showing the main line with the Wansbeck Railway crossing over it, and the B&T station (labelled 'Railway Station') with its line from Newsham. Morpeth's first railway, the Netherton Waggonway (from bottom right), crossing both the Wansbeck and B&T on the level to reach its new staiths adjacent to the main line (prior to the N&B's opening it had extended further west into the town).*

Although the Blyth & Tyne (B&T) was to be vested in the NER on 7 August 1874, at the time of the opening of its branch from Newsham to Morpeth, via Bedlington, it was on far better terms with the North British Railway (NBR). The B&T branch had opened to mineral traffic with a southbound connection on to the NER east of its station on 1 October 1857, but when it opened to passengers, on 1 April 1858, it used its own terminus parallel to the main-line station. When the Wansbeck Railway, which was supported by the NBR, was opened from Scot's Gap to Morpeth on 23 July 1862 it preferred, for ulterior motives, to make its connection with the B&T rather than the easier one with the NER, for which it also had authority. (Figure 6.2)

Richard Hodgson (1812-1877), the NBR chairman, had an obsession to get from Newcastle to Edinburgh without using the Newcastle and Berwick line.[3] As one of his strategies the NBR took over the Wansbeck Railway (of which he was a director) on 21 July 1863. To achieve his objective he could use the B&T's lines from Newcastle to Morpeth, the Wansbeck Railway to Scot's Gap and assist the proposed Northumberland Central Railway (NCR) thence to the NBR near Kelso; this explains the Wansbeck Railway's direct connection to the B&T rather than the NER. The scheme did not work out as the NCR struggled even to complete the 13 miles from Scot's Gap to Rothbury before it ran out of capital. When Hodgson was forced to resign in November 1866, the cash-strapped NBR realized the futility of his schemes in central Northumberland and offered no further help until it took over the Rothbury branch in 1872, two years after its completion.[4] This allowed through NBR services between Morpeth and Rothbury. Had Hodgson's plan worked out Morpeth might have got a third station, at Low Stobhill south of the town, to serve passengers on his somewhat tedious, almost 20-miles longer, through route to Edinburgh. The futility of his whole idea becomes obvious when one recalls that the NBR had got running powers from Newcastle to Hexham in July 1862 giving access to Edinburgh via its own Border Counties and Waverley lines.

Thanks to Hodgson NBR passenger trains using the Wansbeck line had to cross over the main line by a bridge to join the B&T about half-a-mile east of Morpeth, and then had to be propelled in and out of the B&T station. An agreement was made, on 8 August 1871, allowing the NBR a direct connection from the Wansbeck line on to the NER. This was completed by April 1872, but the Board of Trade initially deferred the opening to passengers for one month to allow some signalling to be completed and the NBR to provide a turntable on NER land. However, the NBR was censured when it was found they had started running passenger trains illegally on 3 May, and, although the trains were allowed to continue, final BOT approval was not given until 2 August.[5] NBR passengers would be happy as the new loop reduced the distance from Rothbury to Morpeth by a mile and cut the journey time by eight minutes. In January 1878, the NER let a contract to George Bell, of Gateshead, for £2,926 to provide a passenger subway and to widen the bridge over Shields Road (now A192) to allow an additional track into Morpeth station, which would permit passenger trains from the Wansbeck line access to their new side of the Down platform without occupying the main line.[6] (Plate 6.2) The new island platform face and resignalling were finished in June 1879.[7]

After the NER took over the B&T in 1874, it was obvious that economies could be made by running its services into the NER station. The position of the original N&B goods warehouse, alongside the Up main line, prevented both the extension of the Up platform and the provision of an adjacent bay platform for the use of the former B&T trains. When the warehouse was destroyed by fire, on 1 May 1879, the NER advanced its plans to close the B&T station. On 3 July 1879, the Locomotive Committee approved expenditure of £4,000, which included a new platform, warehouse and re-arranging the signalling to allow trains from Newsham to use the main-line station. The new platform came into use on 24 May 1880 allowing the warehouse to be built on the site of the B&T station's approach tracks (Plate 6.3); the contract was let for £1,467 on 26 May 1880. Also in 1880 a new house was authorized for the permanent way inspector, and the former B&T station was converted into housing for the goods agent and district inspector. (Plate 6.4) The original connection from the Wansbeck to the B&T was abandoned.[8]

Modest covered accommodation for passengers was added as an afterthought to the 1880 changes. A small wooden booking office and waiting room were added to the basic shelter on the Down platform for a mere £95. (Plate 6.5) On 2 December 1880, the traffic committee recommended the removal of 'a large wooden shed' from Fawcett Street, Sunderland, which had recently closed, to the Up platform at Morpeth, 'where extra shelter is needed'. The work of re-erecting it adjacent to the main buildings was carried out in 1881 at a tender price of £110.[9] (Figure 6.3, Plate 6.6) On 19 September 1889 the traffic committee recommended improvements to the station buildings, with an extension to the roof over the Up platform, and, at last, a roof over and additional passenger accommodation on the Down platform. (Plate 6.7) The contract was let to J & W Simpson for £3,294, but the NER had second thoughts and doubled its size, on 7 August 1890, to provide extra platform roofing, passenger and staff accommodation.[10] Only the roofing at the Berwick end of the Up platform has survived modernization and electrification.

In the 1880s the NER ran five through trains, in each direction, on weekdays between Newcastle and Morpeth via Backworth and Newsham, and two trains on Sundays. By the time of the Grouping the through service had reduced to three trains, but five between Newsham and Morpeth and another five between Benton and Morpeth had been added. In LNER days the through trains from Newcastle were altered to terminate at Newbiggin rather than Morpeth, but five still ran each day from Newsham to Morpeth until the service almost disappeared with the onset of the war.

Plate 6.1. *An aerial view of Morpeth taken in the late 1920s showing: (1) cattle mart (2) coal depot (3) old B&T station converted into housing (4) NER goods warehouse of 1880 (5) cattle dock (6) platform used by the former B&T services (7) main station buildings (8) parcels' office (9) Up platform awning (10) Down platform awning (11) loading dock (12) inspector's house (13) locomotive turntable (14) railway housing. (Fred Moffatt)*

Plate 6.2. *An 1878 photograph showing contractor George Bell's workmen completing the temporary works to allow the bridge widening to commence to enable NBR trains to gain access to their own platform at Morpeth station without occupying the Down main. (Harry Horne)*

Plate 6.3. Heaton Class V2 No 60807 heads north from Morpeth on a Whitley Bay to Glasgow train on 14 July 1951. To the left of the train is the Up platform and bay platform for the former B&T trains; the platform on the extreme left is for livestock. The timber building beyond the buffer stops is the parcels office. *(JE Shelbourne / Neville Stead Collection)*

Plate 6.4. The original B&T station converted into housing. *(John F Mallon)*

Plate 6.5. Some of Morpeth's station staff photographed in the 1880s. The basic waiting shelter on the Down platform was little bigger than those provided at the wayside stations; its extension, nearest the camera, was provided in 1880. The hipped-roofed building beyond the shelter is Morpeth's first signal cabin. *(Harry Horne)*

Plate 6.6. Looking towards Berwick along the section of the Up platform covered by the awning recovered from Sunderland in 1881. *(John M Fleming)*

The Rothbury Branch had three weekday trains in each direction, with the first Up and last Down having through coaches to and from Newcastle via the main line until the Second World War. The Beeching axe fell on the passenger service to Newsham on 2 November 1964, but Rothbury had lost its trains as early as 13 September 1952. The Rothbury Branch closed completely on 11 November 1963, and the last goods train ran on the Wansbeck line on 29 September 1966.[11]

Prior to the First World War coal was being transported by rail from over 20 collieries in the Morpeth and Blyth districts (Figure 6.4), but after the Second World War, as the pits closed for political or 'economic' reasons, extensive opencast workings around Widdrington flourished. In order to get the opencast coal to Alcan, at Lynemouth, a new one-mile long curve from the main line north of Morpeth to connect to the Newsham line was opened on 13 May 1980.[12]

Morpeth has seen a recent upsurge in passengers with 226,650 journeys either starting or finishing at the station in 2008/9; an increase of some 20% within two years.[13]

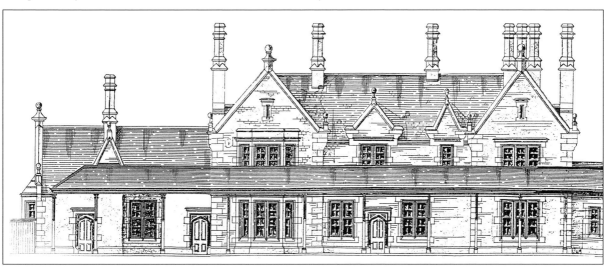

Figure 6.3. Part elevation of Morpeth, dated c.1880, showing the re-used awning from Sunderland in front of the station buildings on the Up platform. (NYMR Archives)

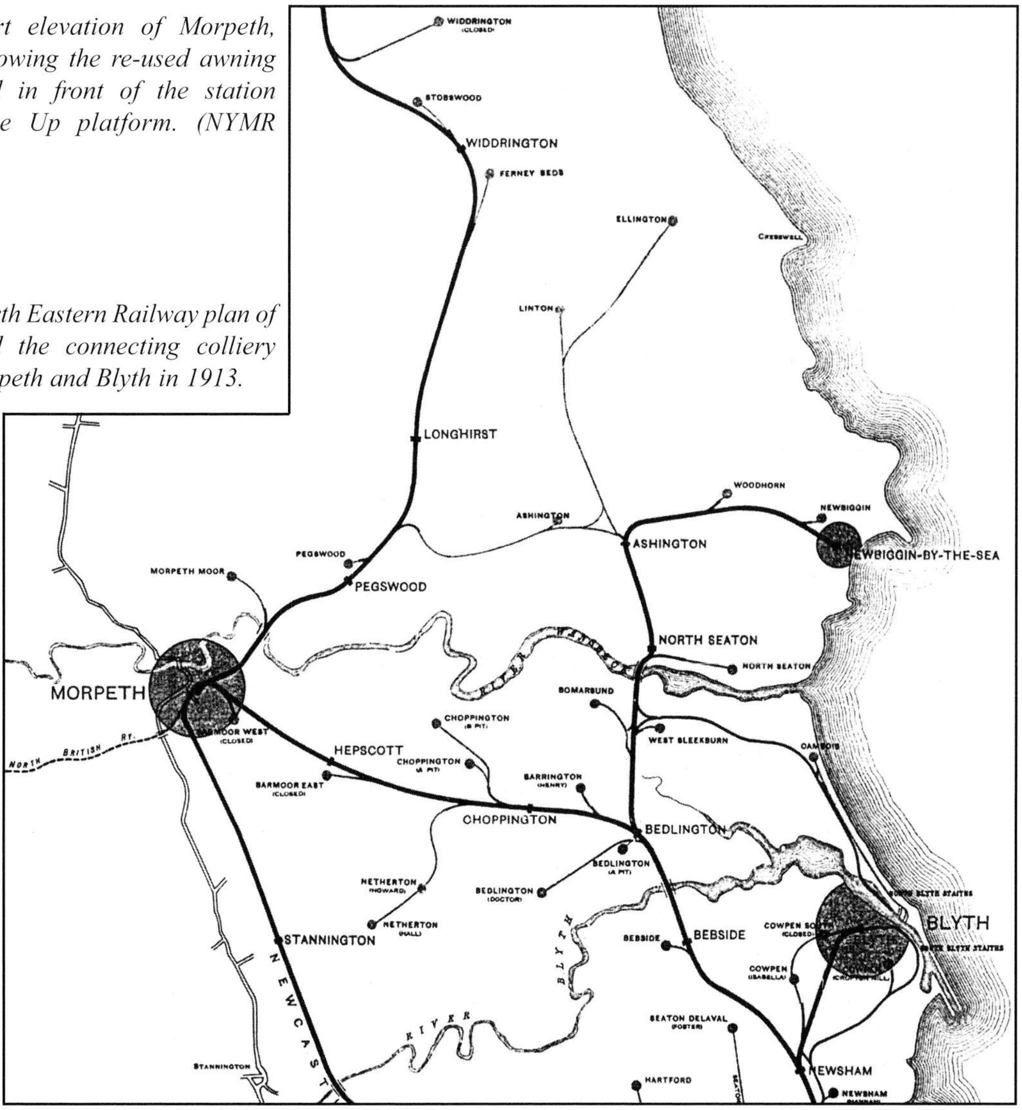

Figure 6.4. A North Eastern Railway plan of its railways and the connecting colliery lines around Morpeth and Blyth in 1913.

Plate 6.7. The 1890 buildings on the Down platform at Morpeth (compare with Plate 6.5), which eventually housed a booking office (right-hand end) permanent way inspector's office, refreshment room, ladies waiting room and a urinal. (Bill Fawcett)

Plate 6.8. An 1880s view of the staff outside the station. (Harry Horne)

Plate 6.9. Morpeth from Newcastle end in July 1905. The widened bridge over the A192 passes under the platform ends. The subway steps are just beyond start of awnings. (Keith Creighton)

Figure 6.5. (Below) A diagram based on Telford's levels showing that, even with summit cuttings and embankments in the valleys, very steep gradients would result if the course of the Great North Road was followed from Morpeth (left) to Alnwick. (Smith-Barlow Report)

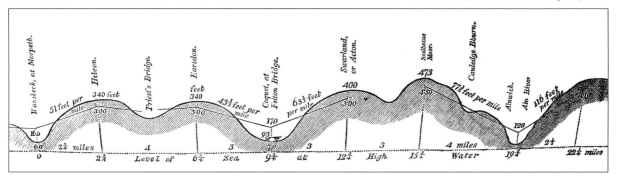

Alnmouth and Alnwick

In 1844 Alnwick (population 6,600), then the county town of Northumberland, though on the Great North Road, was to be 3 miles from both Brunel and Stephenson's main-line railways. When the routes were made public the citizens of Alnwick thought their town was bound to suffer. A public meeting was held on 4 November 1844 'to take into consideration the probable effects of the projected railways, and to adopt measures to defeat any attempt that may be made to carry the railway at a distance from the town, to the manifest injury of its property and trade.' For any measure to succeed in Alnwick it had to have the backing of the Duke of Northumberland. However, when the concerns expressed at the meeting were put to him he was unable to help as 'engineers of the first eminence' had convinced him that it was not possible to take the main line nearer to Alnwick. He was happy for the town to be served by a branch line, but thought that the improvement of the road from the main line at Lesbury 'would be most beneficial to the Town'.[14]

In 1840 a route following Telford's Great North Road, and serving Alnwick, had been shown in the Smith-Barlow report as being too difficult for railway construction. Four miles south of Alnwick the road was over 470 feet above sea level, whereas the projected railways, nearer the coast, were less than 140 feet. Telford's levels (Figure 6.5) indicated that very steep gradients would be needed throughout and, in particular, on each side of the Aln Valley.

The fight for the townspeople was led by the local chemist, William Davison, and they commissioned a survey by civil engineers, John Brunton and John Gandell, to produce a line from Morpeth to Chathill, which passed the town just east of the Duke's ancestral home, Alnwick Castle. (Figure 6.6) Regardless of the fact that it could not solve the gradient problem it was totally objectionable to His Grace, who considered the survey 'a waste of money'.[14] The town's next ploy was to petition the Board of Trade where they got some sympathy from Lord Dalhousie, then its vice-president, and Hudson, in consultation with Robert Stephenson, agreed to add a three-mile branch to the town from Lesbury. This was, to the inhabitants, a poor compromise; had the topography obliged Alnwick would still have a train service. In 1848 plans were deposited for a branch from Bilton to Alnmouth, which was never built. (Figure 6.7)

The main-line station, which became known as Alnmouth from 2 May 1892, has appeared in railway documents and timetables as: Lesbury; Lesbury for Alnwick; Bilton; Bilton Junction. The first temporary station, Lesbury, was nearly a mile north of the present station and was adjacent to the main road from Alnwick to Lesbury and Alnmouth (now A1068). Short temporary platforms at Lesbury were ready for the opening of that section of the line on 1 July 1847, and platform extensions, waiting sheds, a warehouse and omnibus shed were all completed in timber shortly afterwards. The cost of this temporary work came to nearly £1,700, but, as at other locations, it was considered well worthwhile to allow the railway to start earning revenue.[2] The masonry building near the A1068, which still stands, was referred to as 'station house', but unoccupied, in the 1851 census. (Plate 6.10) It had not been completed until early 1849, some 18 months after the main line opened; it was later split into two dwellings for railway employees.

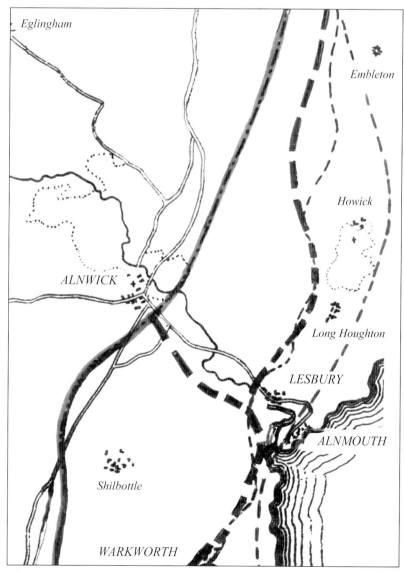

Figure 6.6. *An enlargement of a contemporary plan for the Alnwick area showing: unbroken left – the Brunton-Gandell line; thick dashed – Robert Stephenson's revised line with branch to Alnwick; thin dashed – Brunel's line; extreme right dashed – George Stephenson's original line. (NEIMME)*

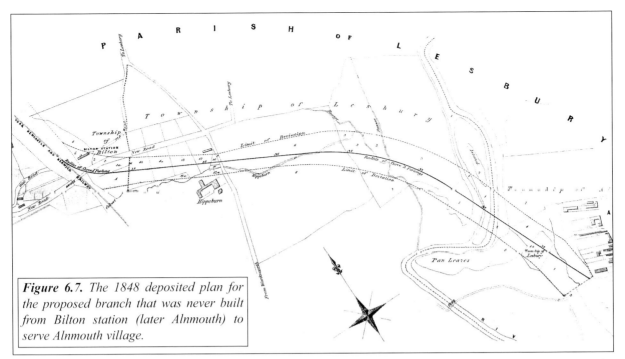

Figure 6.7. *The 1848 deposited plan for the proposed branch that was never built from Bilton station (later Alnmouth) to serve Alnmouth village.*

There is some confusion as to when the station on its present site first opened to passengers; it has been assumed that it coincided with the start of the passenger service on the branch from Alnwick on 1 October 1850. However, the April 1849 timetable, where the Fourth (Parliamentary) Class fares are based on penny-a-mile rates to each station from Carliol Square, Newcastle, suggests that the current location was already in use for both northbound and southbound trains.

Clause 3 in the agreement between Hudson and the third Duke of Northumberland of 26 April 1845, mentioned in Chapter 2, read:

> that there should be a first class station where the Alnwick branch was to join the main trunk line at or near Bilton and that said Company should not take in more land for that station than necessary for the purpose of a first class station, and not for the purpose of erecting granaries, warehouses or other buildings, and that such station should not be made use of as a place for repairing or building engines or for any other purpose than what might be necessary for the ordinary traffic of a railway at a first class station.

The Duke's stipulations and the stark economies following Hudson's downfall in 1849 meant that both Alnmouth and Alnwick got very modest stations. The basic designs, for which the tenders were invited in June 1850, were by the Greens, but it must have crossed their minds that with very little additional money they could have given buildings on a par with the others on the line. However, in the circumstances, economies had to be *seen* to be made to placate the angry shareholders. A station house, identical to Alnwick's, was built on the Up side and basic facilities were provided on each platform. The Down platform had two faces, one to serve the main line and the western one for Alnwick trains.

The third Duke's strictures seemed to have been eased by 1874, and no objections appeared when the NER suggested that an engine shed and cottages for its staff should be built at Alnmouth. The contract for a double-track shed and three cottages was let for £2,090 on 18 April 1875. The shed was to house two locomotives used on the Alnwick branch, and, on 30 June 1887, a tender was accepted for £1,044 to extend it for the two more that were needed to work the new Alnwick & Cornhill (A&C) Branch.[15] (Plate 6.11)

In 1884, as soon as work on the three-year contract for the A&C had begun, the people of Alnwick started to agitate, now with the support of the Duke, for a better station to serve the town. The NER's first reaction was to agree to the request, but in January 1885 the NER Traffic Committee considered it would be better to rebuild the station at Alnmouth. Alnmouth sold fewer tickets than Alnwick, but as a junction station it handled a lot more passengers, and was one of the least imposing stations remaining on the main line, where a continuous series of improvements to facilities was being carried out. However, after further negotiations and deliberations, it was decided to rebuild both stations.[16] Full details and drawings of the old and new stations at Alnwick appear in the late Ken Hoole's *North Eastern Branch Line Termini* (OPC 1985), and a selection of the drawings is repeated in Bart Rippon's *The Alnwick Branch* (Kestrel 2008).

A contract was let on 4 March 1886 for the 'Additions and Improvements' at Alnmouth for £5,525 to J&W Simpson; they later also completed the engine shed extensions and the work at Morpeth in 1890.[17] General, ladies, First Class ladies and gents' waiting rooms and toilets were provided on each platform together with a booking office on the Up platform. A new footbridge and awnings extending over 280 feet in length covered each platform. (Figure 6.8, Plate 6.12) Eight extra cottages for staff were also authorized for £1,415 in March 1887. Alnmouth did not get a goods warehouse or coal cells until the 1886 remodelling; prior to this goods must have been handled at Alnwick

Plate 6.10. The 1849 station house for the temporary Lesbury station. (Bill Fawcett)

Plate 6.11. A 1960 view of Alnmouth shed, the 1887 extension is nearest the camera. The J39 is standing next to the elevated siding, which was authorized in 1890 at a cost of £210, for coaling the locomotives. (Courtesy of Neil and Sue's Picture Framing, Berwick)

and household coal supplied direct from the nearby Shilbottle Colliery. The modest goods warehouse was an enlarged 'three-wagon' version of those used at the seven smaller stations on the A&C[18], and there were only four coal cells; the yard was located on the Up side south of the road overbridge. The other major improvement, prior to the opening of the A&C in September 1887, was the doubling of the line from Alnmouth to Alnwick at a cost of £5,433.[19] A refreshment room was added at the south end of the Down platform in 1900 for £187, and was let to a private operator for a small annual rent (£10 was quoted in 1899 when its cost was estimated at £120).

Like Morpeth, the curve south of Alnmouth viaduct was considered for a major realignment in 1957, which would have bypassed the station to join the existing line some distance further south.[1] The scheme, which would have led to the closure of the station, and only raised the speed of a small number of main-line expresses from 60 to 90 mph, was not considered worth proceeding with. The 1886 buildings started to be demolished in 1980, but it was not until April 1987 that the present building, designed by Mike Tomlinson, was opened.[20] The original 1850 station house survived much of the station for some years as mess rooms for civil engineering staff.

Alnmouth is also seeing a growth in passenger numbers with 197,000 journeys either starting or finishing there in 2009.

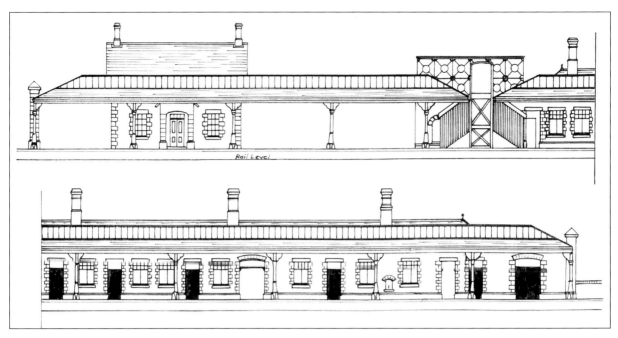

Figure 6.8. The Up platform at Alnmouth showing the 1850 stationmaster's house, the 1858 30,000 gallons water tank and the 1886 awnings, covered footbridge and offices. (JF Addyman)

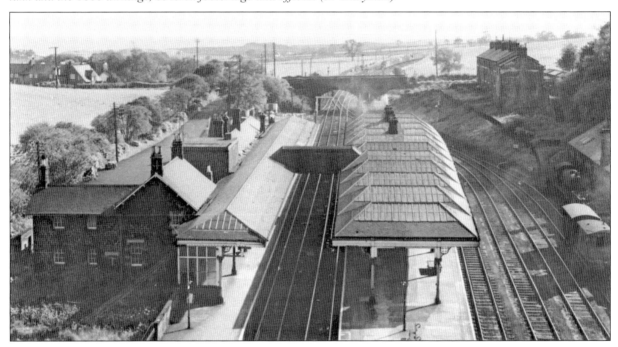

Plate 6.12. A view of Alnmouth taken about 1960 from the very tall signal at the north end of the station. (See also Plate 8.8 on page 82.) Little has changed from the 1886 rebuilding except that the 1850 house (left foreground) has been extended at the rear to provide an additional bedroom. The roof of the goods warehouse can just be seen beyond the road bridge. (Courtesy of Neil and Sue's Picture Framing, Berwick)

Tweedmouth

The Newcastle & Berwick was the last of four railways to reach the mouth of the Tweed, trailing behind the Unthank and Scremerston colliery waggonways and the North British. Coal had been mined in the area for centuries before it finally ceased in 1959. Unthank, three miles SSW of Berwick, was served by a waggonway finishing at a depot in Tweedmouth on the west side of the Great North Road (NT 991523). The N&B crossed the Unthank route on a substantial embankment, pierced by two handsome stone arches, each intended to take a single track. (Plate 6.13) However, it is unlikely that the waggonway ever

occupied these. Though the colliery was working in 1845, its railway was severed by the Kelso Branch construction, and all the many workings at Unthank are shown as abandoned on the 6 inch OS, surveyed in 1860, while the waggonway is not indicated at all. The area was worked in the Twentieth Century, latterly down by the Aller Dean, but with road transport. Nonetheless, parts of the Unthank railway route can still be traced.

Scremerston colliery lay $2^1/_2$ miles SSE of Berwick, on land owned by the Royal Naval Hospital at Greenwich, part of the Derwentwater estates which had been forfeited to the Crown in 1716. Although the pit lay next to the Great North Road, the Hospital Commissioners were enlightened landlords and built a waggonway for their lessees. This ran NNE to the coast at Huds Head and then dropped down an incline from the cliff top to near sea level at the south end of Spittal. (Plate 6.14) It then ran down the main street to a shipping jetty east of the Carr Rock.[21] In 1840, a new shaft, Jack Tar pit, was sunk half a mile south of Scremerston, giving access to better quality coal.[22]

Coal for local sale was taken from the end of the waggonway to Berwick Bridge by means of a rough track along the sands, only usable at low tide. John Grey, who managed the Hospital's 'Northern Estates', therefore persuaded his masters to sanction an extension of their railway to Berwick, and they promoted a parliamentary Bill for this in the session 1844-5. It aroused immense controversy locally, was withdrawn, resubmitted the following year and again withdrawn.[23] The problem was eventually solved by the

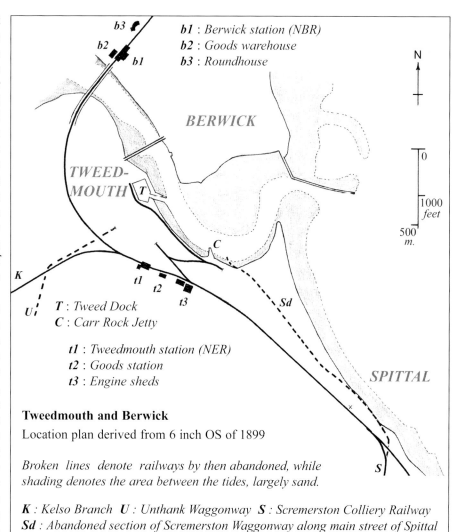

b1 : Berwick station (NBR)
b2 : Goods warehouse
b3 : Roundhouse

T : Tweed Dock
C : Carr Rock Jetty

t1 : Tweedmouth station (NER)
t2 : Goods station
t3 : Engine sheds

Tweedmouth and Berwick

Location plan derived from 6 inch OS of 1899

Broken lines denote railways by then abandoned, while shading denotes the area between the tides, largely sand.

K : Kelso Branch **U** : Unthank Waggonway **S** : Scremerston Colliery Railway
Sd : Abandoned section of Scremerston Waggonway along main street of Spittal

Figure 6.9. Location plan of Berwick and Tweedmouth. (Bill Fawcett)

N&B, which crosses the Scremerston railway about a hundred yards from the top of the Huds Head incline. A north curve was built from the Scremerston line to the N&B and the route east of that was abandoned.[24] The remainder of the line was eventually adapted for locomotive working. Though the colliery has long closed, much remains to be seen, including the beam-engine house of the Jack Tar pit pumping engine (NU 010485). The entire formation of the Scremerston railway survives from there as far as the main line, while the long-abandoned eastern portion is still discernible as a shallow depression as far as the incline head.

The third railway on the scene was the North British, which opened in June 1846 to a station on the site of Berwick Castle. It was a fine building, with a spacious trainshed fronted by an office range in the manner of a castellated villa. (Plate 6.15) Within six years there were two goods warehouses there, while locomotives were catered for at a 12-stall half-roundhouse to the north of the over-bridge carrying the Great North Road.[25] In a sensible world, the N&B would have shared Berwick station while providing its own warehouse and engine stabling in Tweedmouth. However, Hudson was piqued by North British

resistance to his moves for a takeover, and so provided a second, quite needless station in Tweedmouth, a mile from the centre of Berwick. Hudson was determined to make a show, and so Benjamin Green went to town with the finest of all his stations, one with a slightly later, more Jacobean flavour than the others, thanks to its display of shaped gables and an arched portico. (Plate 6.16 and Figure 6.11)

Tweedmouth station had two platforms, flanking four tracks and covered by a trainshed with two spans of 'Euston' style roofing. (Figure 6.10) Adopting two spans enabled Green to use a fairly steep roof pitch so as to harmonise with the frontage building, as Hudson's favourite architect, GT Andrews, had done earlier at Richmond. Unfortunately, no details survive of the, presumably decorative, gable screens of the roof. This was fronted by a one-storey office building, with a two-storey range projecting at right angles and providing a picturesque sense of enclosure to the forecourt. The N&B did not build a house for the Tweedmouth stationmaster, though one wonders if he was originally intended to occupy part of the two-storey block, which in fact opened as a hotel and refreshment rooms.[26] (Plate 6.17)

Plate 6.13. Arches intended to admit the Unthank waggonway through the high embankment carrying the N&B main line but evidently never used. View from south-west. (John F Addyman, 2009)

Plate 6.14. Scremerston waggonway in the 1820s.

Plate 6.15. The North British Railway's Berwick station was a castellated villa, seen here in the early nineteen-hundreds about twenty years before it was replaced by the present building. (Neil and Sue's Picture Framing, Berwick)

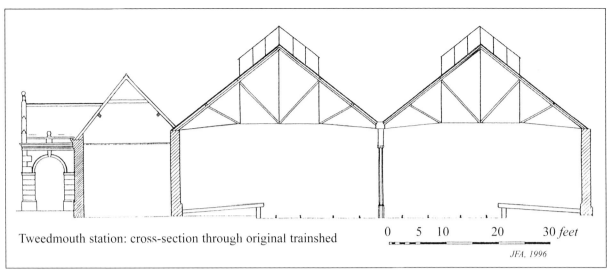

Tweedmouth station: cross-section through original trainshed

0 5 10 20 30 *feet*

JFA, 1996

Figure 6.10. *A cross-section showing the twin-span trainshed at Tweedmouth which was replaced by awnings in 1906. (JF Addyman, 1996)*

Plate 6.16. *The handsome portico of Benjamin Green's Tweedmouth station was more Jacobean in character than his other stations. The former hotel juts out behind it to the left. (John M Fleming, 1966)*

Plate 6.17. *The view from the north-west showing the former hotel with its fine array of shaped gables. (John M Fleming, 1966)*

61

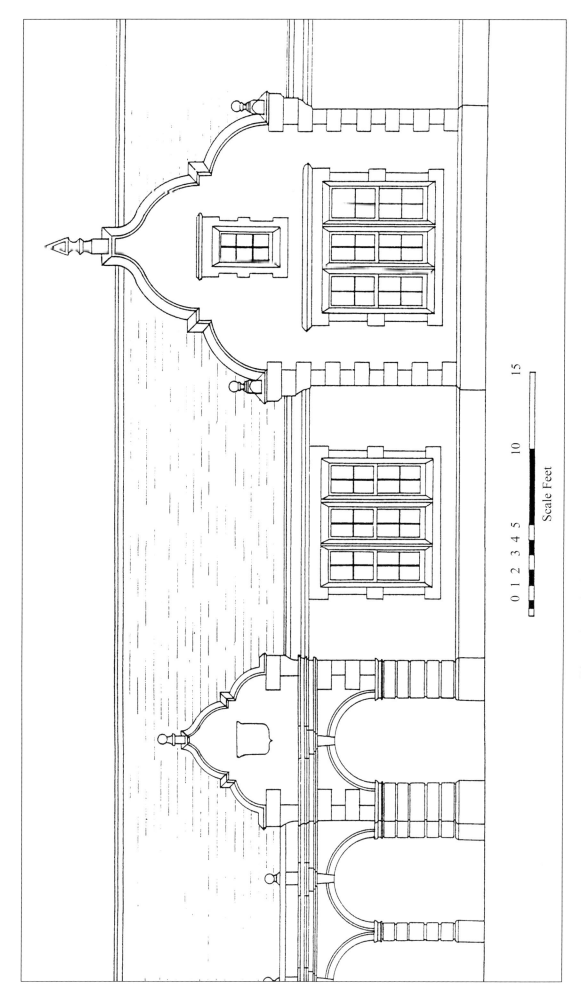

Figure 6.11. *The frontage of Tweedmouth station. (John F Addyman)*

0 1 2 3 4 5   10   15

Scale Feet

Accompanying the station was a terrace of dwellings, in matching style. (Plate 6.18) This was the only such example to be found on the original N&B, and housed men working at the nearby engine shed – a four-road straight shed, accompanied by a low workshop range, kitted out in gothic fashion to blend with the station. It was an essay in the same manner as the goods sheds, and Tweedmouth possessed the largest of these, equipped with no less than three cart bays. There were only 12 houses in the terrace but already, by 1849, the shed was manned by eight drivers and eight firemen.[27]

The engine shed proved to be the most important feature of the railway scene at Tweedmouth, since this long remained a changeover point for locomotives on goods and stopping trains. (Plates 6.19, 6.20) A second shed was built during 1877-8, and this was a typical NER 'square roundhouse' with 20 roads radiating from one turntable.[28] (Plate 6.22) Tweedmouth was important enough to warrant a proper coaling stage (Plate 6.21), while increasingly thirsty engines were catered for by constructing a reservoir and pumping station over a mile away at East Ord, from which water was piped alongside the Kelso Branch. The growing numbers of enginemen were not matched by additional housing until 1900, when the company built Howick Terrace and Falloden [sic] Terrace to a good standard design by the NER Architect, William Bell.[29] Figure

6.14 shows the extent of the station area by the 1920s.

The houses occupy spare land sloping down to the NER's Tweed Dock Branch, a very idiosyncratic line. Berwick had been Scotland's leading port prior to the Wars of Independence, and continued to play a significant role in later, more peaceful centuries. Trading ships used the Town Quay, just outside the Elizabethan town walls, but the deep-water berth was at the Carr Rock, on the south bank. An Act of 1808 set up the Berwick Harbour Commissioners to take over management of the port from the mayor and burgesses, and in 1870 they approached the NER with a proposal to build a dock at Tweedmouth.[30] The NER declined to invest in the venture but agreed to build a connecting railway. The Berwick Harbour Act of May 1872 allowed the commissioners to build the Tweed Dock and to reclaim and embank the foreshore from Berwick Bridge to Carr Rock, with provision for forming a road along this land, linking Berwick with Spittal; it also provided a route for the lower part of the Dock Branch railway. The dock, engineered by that notable Edinburgh dynasty: the Stevensons, cost £90,000 and saw its first vessels in August 1876, with the formal opening on 4 October.[31] It remains in use today, in a very modest way, when so many others have closed to commercial traffic. (Front Cover) The gates have been removed, making it tidal but accessible to broader vessels than those originally catered for.

Plate 6.18. The enginemen's terrace at Tweedmouth, carefully designed by Green to match the station buildings. (JC Dean, 1966)

Figure 6.12. Tweedmouth from 1851 Ordnance Survey.

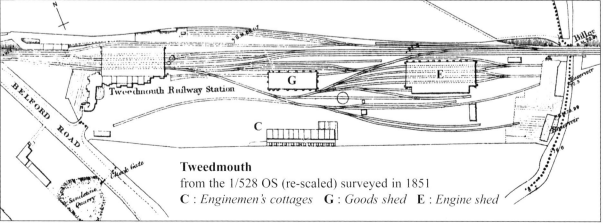

Tweedmouth
from the 1/528 OS (re-scaled) surveyed in 1851
C : *Enginemen's cottages* **G** : *Goods shed* **E** : *Engine shed*

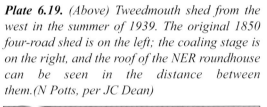

Plate 6.19. (Above) Tweedmouth shed from the west in the summer of 1939. The original 1850 four-road shed is on the left; the coaling stage is on the right, and the roof of the NER roundhouse can be seen in the distance between them.(N Potts, per JC Dean)

Plate 6.20. (Above) The original workshop range attached to the 1850 engine shed. (JC Dean, 1966)

Plate 6.21. (Right) Tweedmouth coaling stage.

Plate 6.22. (Below) The NER roundhouse of 1877-8, seen from the south-east, is one of the last surviving examples of its type at the time of writing. (JC Dean, 1968)

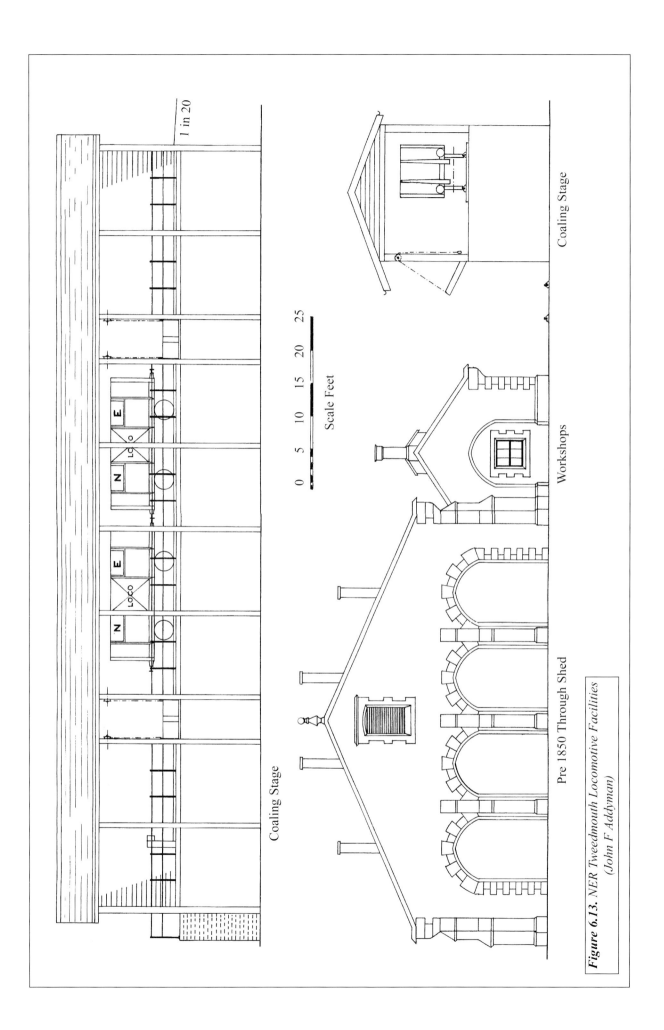

1 in 20

Coaling Stage

Coaling Stage

25

20

15

10

5

0

Scale Feet

Coaling Stage

Workshops

Pre 1850 Through Shed

Figure 6.13. NER Tweedmouth Locomotive Facilities
(John F Addyman)

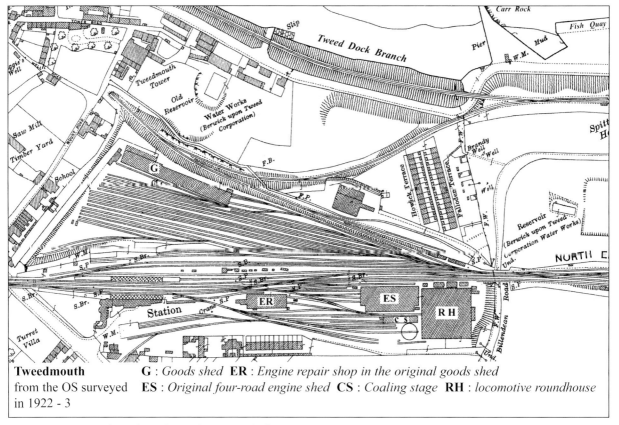

Tweedmouth

from the OS surveyed
in 1922 - 3

G : *Goods shed* **ER** : *Engine repair shop in the original goods shed*

ES : *Original four-road engine shed* **CS** : *Coaling stage* **RH** : *locomotive roundhouse*

Figure 6.14. Tweedmouth in the early 1920s (Ordnance Survey)

The NER went to Parliament in the session 1873-4 with proposals for a dock branch leaving the main line at the south end of Spittal and then dropping at a steady 1 in 53 gradient.[32] This was opposed and dropped – householders on the west side of Spittal High Street cannot have welcomed a railway at first-floor level passing the bottom of their gardens. The following year, the NER came back with a scheme which was approved, for a line dropping straight down from Tweedmouth to the dock. The term straight is illusory. The line had to lose a lot of height in a short distance, so TE Harrison was obliged to devise a zig-zag, with three straight portions – gradient 1 in 50 – linked by two reversals. The railway contract was not let until July 1876 and it opened on 16 October 1878.

Tweedmouth station enjoyed but a brief period of glory before its relegation to an infrequent service of Kelso Branch and main-line stopping trains. (Plate 6.23) An indication of its true utility is provided by the fact that when the NER planned to close the refreshment room a petition against this was received from their own enginemen. Clearly, it was a valuable adjunct to the shed, though of little use to anyone else, and it survived at least until the First World War. The station survived until its eventual closure in 1964 unscathed, save for the 1906 replacement of the trainshed roof by a pair of platform awnings. (Plate 6.24)

The formation of the LNER at the start of 1923 brought scope for rationalisation, leading to the closure of the North British engine shed the following year. That enabled the railway to remodel the tracks in the vicinity of Berwick station and embark on a reconstruction originally planned by the North British

in 1914 but deferred on account of the war. The present station was completed in 1927, and is well organised with an island platform bearing a range of handsome wooden buildings under a glazed roof. These originally included dining and refreshment rooms, which were still functioning in the nineteen-sixties though by then in private hands.

The engine sheds dominated the railway scene at Tweedmouth, and the NER reorganized its layout to make more space for the locomotive department. Thus in 1902-3 they built a new goods shed on the seaward side of the tracks at the station, and in 1907 they converted the original goods shed into a repair shop; part of it also became home to the engineer's breakdown crane.[33] In August 1924, Tweedmouth gained the 21 engines stabled at Berwick shed but in March 1939 it lost half its stock through the closure of Berwick marshalling yard, which meant that goods trains between Newcastle and Edinburgh no longer swapped engines at Tweedmouth, though their crews continued to change there. Tweedmouth shed still boasted 31 locomotives in 1954, but the introduction of diesel traction soon put it out of work, and it closed in June 1966, after which the only engine based at Tweedmouth was a diesel shunter.

The nineteen-sixties saw the end of Tweedmouth as a railway centre, with the loss of passenger services in 1964 and the closure of the Kelso Branch to goods the next year, the Dock Branch having already closed. All the buildings there were destroyed with the exception of the 1878 roundhouse, which was taken over by the builders' merchants, JT Dove, who occupy the rest of the site. Even the roundhouse is now out of use, but still stands despite serious fire damage to its roof. Apart from the main line and the signal box at the former Kelso Branch junction, the railway presence is limited to a few sidings for the use of the civil engineer. Over at East Ord, the site of the locomotive reservoir is now home to Berwick Garden Centre.

Endnotes:

1. One of the authors was involved in surveying the coeval Alnmouth realignment scheme in November 1957.

2. National Archives RAIL 772/52.

3. Addyman JF and Mallon JF. *The Alnwick & Cornhill Railway* (2007) pp 6-7.

4. *Ibid* p 11.

5. National Archives MT6/87/8. On 12 April 1872 when Lieutenant Colonel (later Major General) CS Hutchinson (1826-1912) inspected the double-track loop on behalf of the BOT he found the signalling incomplete, and that B&T would no longer allow the NBR the use of its turntable. He deferred the opening for a month to allow the signalling to be completed, and required the NBR to provide a new turntable. He later found that they had started to run passenger trains from 3 May 1872 without the turntable and, therefore, BOT approval. The NBR were then given until 31 July to provide the turntable on NER land; this was done and final approval was given on 2 August. Cook and Hoole *NER Historical Maps* (1991) p 25, usually an extremely reliable source, give

the loop opening to goods traffic on 3 May 1872 but not opening to passengers until 24 May 1880 *i.e.* the same day as the former B&T trains started to use the main-line station; this is obviously incorrect. Warn CR *Main Line Railways of Northumberland* (1976) p 35 inevitably confuses the issue: 'A curve between the Wansbeck Railway and the NER line was made at joint expense and a third station, Morpeth NBR, opened in 1872 on the north side. This involved widening the bridge over the A192… Once the B&T was amalgamated into the NER in 1874, the old B&T station was relegated to parcels and freight.'

6. NER Locomotive Committee minutes 18399 20 December 1877 and 18453 17 January 1878 (National Archives RAIL 527/33).

7. National Archives MT6/233/9. Major General Hutchinson approved these alterations on 4 July 1879. The plans submitted show that the loop to the Wansbeck line, which was double in 1872, had already been singled, and that the old connection to the former B&T was still in situ, but not signalled.

8. NER Traffic Committee minutes: 12128 8 May 1879; 12172 19 June 1880; 12389 24 March 1880; 12578 4 November 1880 (National Archives RAIL 527/68). Locomotive Committee minutes: 19766 3 July 1879; 19838 17 July 1879; 19856 31 July 1879; 20581 26 May 1880 (National Archives RAIL 527/34-5).

Plate 6.23. *An overall view of Tweedmouth, with the station in the background and the goods shed, adapted for locomotive repairs, on the right. The Class 40 locomotive was handling freight trains there in the final years of the shed's existence. (John M Fleming, 1966)*

Plate 6.24. *Tweedmouth station from the west showing the verandahs which replaced the original trainshed in 1906. (Neil and Sue's Picture Framing, Berwick)*

9. NER Locomotive Committee minutes: 20655 3 June 1880; 21188 2 December 1880; 21867 28 July 1881 (National Archives RAIL 527/35).

10. NER Way and Works Committee minutes: 5100 19 September 1889; 5685 3 July 1890; 5760 7 August 1890 (National Archives RAIL 527/40).

11. Sewell GWM. *The North British Railway in Northumberland* (1992) p 128.

12. In 1882 the NER sought approval to build an 11 chains (220m) radius 'north' to east curve at Morpeth and a nine chains (180m) west to north curve at Newsham, but did not proceed with either of them.

13. Office of Rail Regulation

14. Report of the Alnwick Railway Committee 27 January 1845. NEIMME.

15. Hoole, K. *North Eastern Locomotive Sheds* (1972) p 28.

16. A&C pp 45-7.

17. NER Way & Works Committee 30 June 1887 minute 3611 and 1 December 1887 minute 3078 (National Archives RAIL 527/40).

18. A&C p 57. Unlike most other stations on the main line it did not provide covered accommodation for loading or unloading the carts and wagons.

19. Board Minute 9466 (National Archives RAIL 527/17).

20. Fawcett W. *A History of NER Architecture Volume 3* (2005) pp 229, 234.

21. National Archives ADM 76/74 is a box of Greenwich Hospital papers relating to the 1843-5 schemes for the extension of the Scremerston line to the south end of Berwick Bridge. These include plans showing the original route along Spittal main street to the jetty.

22. NEIMME, 3410/Bell/19/9 & 11 re Scremerston Colliery. 3410/Bell/19/517 re Unthank Colliery.

23. National Archives ADM 76/74 contains the Deposited Plans of November 1843 and November 1844 with related papers. House of Commons Journal reports consent being given on 27 June 1845 for the withdrawal of the Bill. Some newspaper reports filed in Bell (note 22) indicate virulent antagonism towards the scheme. Some was based on fears, which the hospital tried to allay, that their railway would cut off access to the foreshore.

24. There was only a small height difference between the waggonway and main line at their crossing, but it is possible that the eastern end remained open for a while after the opening of the N&B. It had been abandoned prior to the 1860 survey for the 6-inch OS.

25. 1851 1/528 OS of Berwick. *Railway Magazine*, June 1909, pp 473-8, features Berwick as a 'Notable Railway Station' and gives useful information and pictures.

26. Directories and large-scale maps confirm the usage of the building.

27. NER Tweedmouth: *Chronological Record of Engine Drivers, Firemen, Cleaners etc. from the Year 1848*. Private collection.

28. NER Locomotive & Works Committee 8 November 1877 let the roundhouse contract at £6,987-12-3 to Thomas Watson of Jarrow. On 18 July 1878 they confirmed its transfer to his sureties, with the roof ironwork going to Close of York. (National Archives RAIL 527/33)

29. NER Way & Works Committee 20 March 1902 let the contract. The houses rents were set at 5s per week inclusive of rates and taxes. (National Archives RAIL 527/45)

30. NER Locomotive & Works Committee 18 November 1870; 7 November 1871 (National Archives RAIL 527/28).

31. The entrance was hurriedly dredged to let in four vessels on 19 August, after which the dock was unused and fitting out continued until the formal opening.

32. Northumberland Archives, Woodhorn, have the Deposited Plans of November 1873 and 1874 for the two schemes in accession QRUp.

33. Hoole K, *North Eastern Locomotive Sheds*, pp 49-53 gives valuable details of locomotive allocations and workings at Tweedmouth. NER Way & Works Committee 25 February 1907 authorised the conversion of the goods shed (National Archives RAIL 527/48).

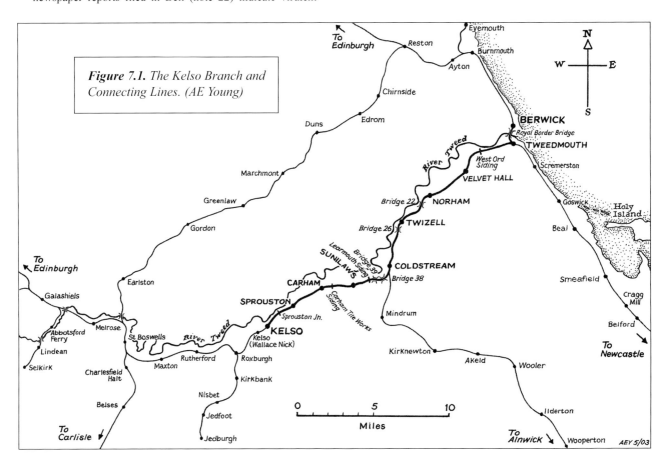

Figure 7.1. The Kelso Branch and Connecting Lines. (AE Young)

Chapter 7 : The Kelso Branch

Christopher Dean[1]

Planning and Building the Line

Although there were turnpike roads on both sides of the River Tweed a scheme was considered to join Kelso with the coast by a 'Line of Iron' as early as 1806. John Rennie FRS (1761-1821), who had already completed the Tweed Bridge at Kelso in 1804, was asked to report on the proposed 'Rail-Way' in 1809; this culminated in the passing of the Berwick & Kelso Railway Act on 31 May 1811 [2] This was not the first Act of Parliament for a railway, but it is claimed to be the first to contain a clause permitting the conveyance of passengers. Obviously, with it being promoted within the decade of the world's first steam locomotive having run, it was planned to use horses for moving passengers and goods. The economic advantages of using rails rather than roads had been amply demonstrated in the coalfields by that time – one horse on a waggonway could move as much as 25 packhorses on the roads.

The line was to commence at Spittal, a small town at the mouth of the Tweed opposite Berwick, and to terminate in Kelso after crossing the Tweed at Twizell.[3] The issued share capital of the company was to be £100,000, coupled with powers to raise a further £50,000 by means of loans. Nothing came of these plans, although the proprietors tried to revive their railway in the 1820s and again in the early 1830s, when they had the support of Sir Walter Scott of Abbotsford and other local businessmen.

The Great North British Railway proposal of 1839 made no provision for a branch to Kelso, but both the Stephenson and Brunel schemes of 1844 included one from Tweedmouth. The Stephenson plan had a facing junction from the Newcastle direction but the other proposed one from Edinburgh; both railways kept to the south of the Tweed throughout. The Kelso Branch, the longest of three authorized by the Newcastle & Berwick Act of 31 July 1845, was something of a misnomer in as much as it was not planned to go into Kelso, but to terminate on the south bank of the river opposite the town. Here it was intended to make an end-on junction with the NBR's line from St Boswells, on what was to become the 'Waverley Route'.[4] The length of the branch was to be 21³/₄ miles, but it ended up with the NBR completing the final half-a-mile. Although the NBR line had been authorized in June 1846 it was not able to link up with the YN&B at Mellendean Farm (known as Sprouston Junction) until 1 June 1851. Due to problems with the NBR's alignment around Kelso it had to use a temporary terminus south-west of the town for most of the previous year.

The Tweed valley gave access to the lowland Scottish woollen industry, which lay between Hawick and Galashiels. The valley was particularly fertile, and all types of farming were practised there. The opening of the Edinburgh to Hawick line in 1849 and the completion of the Kelso branches in 1851 gave the area rail links to the north and east, but it was not until 1862 that the Border Union Railway completed the 'Waverley Route' to Carlisle, giving access to the WCML and north-west England.

Two tenders were invited for building the N&B Kelso Branch on 25 January 1847; the first from Tweedmouth to Oxendean Burn (near Donaldson's Lodge, 11¹/₄ miles) and the second from there to Sprouston (10 miles). Both contracts were let initially for a total of £220,000 to Messrs Morris and Wilcocks who were civil engineers working for the Edinburgh & Glasgow Railway. Soon the partnership was dissolved, and Robert Morris – presumably anxious to reduce his commitments – only retained the Tweedmouth contract, and the Kelso one was re-let to William Hutchinson (*circa* 1801-1874).[5]

Each contract included two masonry viaducts. On the Tweedmouth contract the first crossed a stream in the Newbiggin Dene, 7¹/₂ miles from Tweedmouth, and the second the River Till 2¹/₂ miles further on; both had six segmental arches of 52 feet 6 inch span. (Plate 7.1) On the Kelso contract each viaduct crossed both a stream and a public road at East and West Learmouth with semi-circular arches. East Learmouth with five skew-spans of 42 feet 0 inch was a mile south of Cornhill (Coldstream) station. (Plate 7.2) West Learmouth, half-a-mile further west, had seven spans of 36 feet 6 inch.[6] The Till viaduct was not quite complete when Captain (later Colonel) HG Wynne, RE, inspected the line on 23 July 1849 as there had been problems with the foundations; he agreed to the use of the single-track temporary viaduct with the precaution that 'all trains should pass very slowly over the timber bridge'.[7] Appendix 2 gives the mileages of the main features on the branch.

Plate 7.1. *The River Till viaduct (Bridge No 26) with its six flat segmental arches. (JC Dean, 1966)*

Plate 7.2. *East Learmouth viaduct with its five semi-circular arches. (JC Dean, 1969)*

Figure 7.2. *Velvet Hall station house as extended in 1905. (JF Addyman)*

Platform Elevation

Approach Elevation

Store	General Waiting Room		Kitchen	Urinal
Pump				EC
WC	Ladies' Room	Booking and Parcels Office	Scullery	EC
				Coals

Ground Plan

Scale feet

0 5 10 15 20 25 30

Plate 7.3. *Norham, looking towards Tweedmouth circa 1900. The building in the centre is the upper floor of the stationmaster's house. The signal cabin dates from the introduction of the block system in about 1880; note the oval Telegraph Fault Sign Board. Similar cabins appear to have been erected at the other stations on the branch, with Twizell and Velvet Hall lasting until final closure. The window design, the angled boarding below the windows, and the provision of a stove rather than a brick chimney stack were unusual features for the Northern Division, with the only similarity to other contemporary cabins being the pitched roof. (JC Dean Collection)*

Plate 7.4. Norham, looking towards Coldstream, showing the additional wooden building next to the stationmaster's house and the replacement signal box of 1902. (Lens of Sutton Association)

The branch was double track and had an initial total of 53 bridges and culverts; a footbridge was added at Coldstream station following the opening of the line from Alnwick in 1887. Nearly all the bridges were masonry with segmental arches, but four, over highways, were constructed with wrought-iron girders to provide more clearance for the road traffic. The branch crossed the Scottish border at 17.65 miles from its junction with the Newcastle & Berwick, making it the only line owned by an English company to have two stations in Scotland (Carham and Sprouston). The actual border was marked by the LNER who erected their usual steel ENGLAND/SCOTLAND sign.

Stations and Other Facilities

The contracts for the stations were let on 27 January 1849, and their designs were by the Newcastle architects, John and Benjamin Green, who had produced the much more elegant buildings on the main line (See Chapter 5). Sanderson & Company of Amble were engaged to build the stations at Sprouston and Cornhill (and possibly Carham and Sunilaws), whilst Armstrong & Hudspeth had made the successful bid for Velvet Hall and Norham.[8] The *Berwick Advertiser* reported that the branch should be open in May 1849, but as was usual, Press and directors' reports tended to be optimistic. The branch did open for traffic as far as Sprouston station on 27 July 1849, the first train leaving Tweedmouth at 7.30 am.

When the line opened there were stations at Velvet Hall, Norham, Cornhill, Carham and Sprouston. A temporary station at Wark was replaced by a permanent one (renamed Sunilaws in 1871) which opened in January 1851; the station at Twizell opened in August 1861. The undulating terrain, and the fact that the line was built as part of a direct route to serve the upper-Tweed valley meant none of the intermediate stations was well sited for would-be passengers. Velvet Hall – so called after an adjacent farm – was over a mile from the nearest village, Horncliffe. Norham village was nearly a mile from its station, and Twizell served a scattered population of fewer than 200, but had the highest usage on the line with 20 journeys per person per annum (Carham and Sprouston served a total population of 1,500, but only generated five journeys

per head). There is a small village at Cornhill, but the much larger Scottish town of Coldstream is over a mile distant on the other side of the Tweed. Similarly, because of problems with the Duke of Roxburghe, the North British station for Kelso was almost a mile away across the Tweed at Maxwellheugh.

Whilst the stations possessed a certain rural charm, their appearance had little in common with each other. It is quite likely that there were cutbacks in expenditure even prior to the imminent fall from grace of the YN&BR chairman, George Hudson. This may explain their simple and varied design; however, all were stone-built with slate-roofs. Velvet Hall was a two-storey, plain looking building combining the offices and stationmaster's house under one roof. In order to increase the accommodation for the stationmaster and his family the house was subsequently extended – most recently in 1905. (Colour Plate 8 and Figure 7.2) The original portion of the building contained some pleasing mullioned windows – those on the first floor being dormers.

When the line had reached Norham it was running along an embankment, with the result that the first floor windows of the stationmaster's house looked out on to the Down platform, whilst the ground floor was level with the road and station approach. The shape of the building was not dissimilar to Velvet Hall when seen from the road, but the eaves were unbroken, with the first floor windows below the roofline. Later the overall impression of the station, when seen from platform level, was somewhat spoiled by a hotchpotch of stone and wooden buildings – a reflection of development over a period. (Plates 7.3, 7.4) Twizell, opened more than a decade after the rest of the branch as a request stop, had a very basic, small, single-storey building with a wooden extension alongside. (Plate 7.5)

Cornhill, renamed Coldstream in 1873, serving a population of over 3,000 was the most important station on the branch, and was a much more impressive affair when viewed from the platforms. (Plates 7.6, 7.7) The elevation from the road side, even with its mullioned windows, was somewhat austere. (Plate 7.8) The stationmaster's house was on two floors and attached to the station offices which were single-storey.

Plate 7.5. Twizell, looking towards Tweedmouth on 26 April 1952, still with its original 1880 signal box. *(JW Armstrong / Armstrong Railway Photographic Trust)*

Plate 7.6. Coldstream, looking towards Kelso in the 1940s. The stationmaster's house and offices are on the right, and the A697 crosses under the railway at the end of the platforms. The Alnwick & Cornhill branches off to the left soon after it crosses the road. *(JC Dean collection)*

Plate 7.7. A view of Coldstream looking towards Tweedmouth. The footbridge and signal box date from the opening of the Alnwick & Cornhill Branch in 1887. *(NERA Collection)*

Plate 7.8. Another view of Coldstream station, this one taken in 1963 from the approach road. *(Courtesy RM Casserley)*

Plate 7.9. *Carham station looking towards Kelso. (JC Dean Collection)*

Plate 7.10. *A general view of Sprouston looking towards Tweedmouth in 1952. The disused engine shed is in the centre of the picture. (JW Armstrong / Armstrong Railway Photographic Trust)*

The booking office was something of a gem, with a bay window looking out over the platform surmounted by a triangular gable containing the station clock. This bay window feature, which was seen on many of the stations on the N&B main line, was encountered again at Sprouston.

There was a basic similarity between Sunilaws and Carham; both had two-storey houses with dormer windows; Sunilaws had a two-storey additional building whereas Carham's extension was single storey. (Plate 7.9) At both the platforms were staggered on each side of a public level crossing. Sprouston, like Coldstream, was of a more attractive design, no doubt due to it being the last station on the branch. Whilst not so extensive, it sported a similar bay-windowed booking office, but the stationmaster's house had its gable end on to the platform; mullioned windows were again used. (Plate 7.10)

All the stations were provided with waiting shelters on the platform opposite the main buildings; Coldstream and Sprouston had masonry fronts, but all the others were of timber in typical NER styles. From the outset the usual cottages were provided throughout the line for gate-keepers and other railway employees, and several additional ones were built during the 1880s and 90s. Four at Cornhill, built in 1897, resulted in the NER being convicted by the local magistrates for building them without local authority approval!

The facilities for handling goods traffic ranged from basic siding accommodation only at Twizell and Learmouth Siding to Velvet Hall, Norham and Coldstream having warehouses, loading docks for livestock and machinery as well as coal and lime cells. Specimen figures for 1913 and 1923 show that the branch handled around 7,000 tons of grain each year and over 2,000 wagons of livestock. More than half the livestock was handled at Coldstream where there was a thriving cattle mart. Up to 1,000 tons of potatoes and beet could be forwarded in a good year, and small quantities of timber and quarried stone were also handled.[9] The sale of coal from the depots at all the stations except Carham and Twizell helped to enhance the stationmasters' salaries – a common practice on the NER. Learmouth Siding also had four coal cells, and there was a private siding serving a tile works straddling the border near Carham. There was a small public delivery siding at West Ord on the Up line but this was moved to the Down side of the branch during 1935.

The 1865 OS map shews that there was a siding to a gravel pit on the Down line about 1500 yards south of Coldstream station, at Grid Ref NT 860382. The siding was also shewn on the 1884 OS together with a trailing cross over, but not on that for 1898. No evidence has been found of the signalling arrangements.

Most North Eastern termini had engine stabling facilities, and Sprouston was no exception. The first shed was a timber one erected in 1863, which came second-hand from the Newcastle & Carlisle Railway.

It blew down on 14 October 1881, and was replaced during 1882 by a single-road, brick building which could house one locomotive. The shed closed in 1916 as an economy measure, but was used to store the preserved Great Western *City of Truro* during the Second World War. The shed remained empty after the locomotive was returned to the York Railway Museum in 1947, but was not demolished until the mid-1960s.[10]

Locomotive water columns were provided in the 1860s for the Up and Down directions at Sprouston and Coldstream stations. The columns were served via the normal NER standard cast-iron storage tanks of 6,800 and 17,000 gallons capacity, respectively. Sprouston tank was fed by surface water drainage, and Coldstream's supply was pumped from springs in a quarry near Cramond Hill, some 500 yards north-east of the station. A Cowans, Sheldon 50 feet diameter turntable was installed at Coldstream to coincide with the opening of the line from Alnwick in 1887.[11]

Captain Wynne's report for the opening of the branch referred to signals being in place at all the stations.[7] As signal boxes were virtually unknown in the north-east, at that time, the points and signals would have been worked individually by the station staff as few of these would be remotely controlled even from a lever frame. In 1871, when the NER eventually realised that block signalling would go a long way towards improving its lamentable safety record, the Kelso Branch did not rate high on its priorities. The branch did not get block signalling together with the necessary signal boxes until 1880, and the late start meant that it did not get the standard NER Northern Division signal boxes that were used on most other lines.[12] Velvet Hall and Twizell were predominately timber structures set on stone and brick bases respectively.[13] Norham was similar at first, when it formed part of the main range of buildings on the Down platform, but it was replaced by a new Northern Division standard cabin (N4) at the west end of the Up platform in 1902. The earlier boxes at Sunilaws, Carham and Sprouston were probably similar to Velvet Hall and Twizell, and were replaced by standard ones between 1901 and 1912. The new cabin at Coldstream station dated from the opening of the Alnwick & Cornhill line in 1887, and was of the earlier Northern Division (N2) style. The cabin at Learmouth Siding, midway between Coldstream and Sunilaws, was replaced by a ground frame in 1907, and Coldstream South (which signalled the Alnwick & Cornhill Branch only) and Tweedmouth West closed in 1904 and 1906 respectively. (See Appendix 3B.)

Passenger Services

Although the main passenger services on the branch were between Berwick and Kelso, a reversal was needed due to the junction on to the branch facing south; this required the locomotive to run round its train at Tweedmouth. The initial service was three trains each way on weekdays between Berwick and Sprouston, and two on Sundays. First and Second Class passengers were carried on all trains but Third Class ones only on the first train on each weekday (on both on Sundays). A horse-bus carried passengers between Sprouston and Kelso until the connection with the

NBR line was achieved. By 1858 there was an additional train each way on weekdays, but still only the first train of the day could be used by 'Parliamentary Class' passengers, though the last train of the day was available to Third Class. The fares were:

First	4s 9d (24p)
Second	4s 0d (20p)
Third	2s 6d (12.5p)
Parliamentary	1s 11½d (10p)

By 1881 the distinction between Third and Parliamentary Classes had been removed, and the fares were reduced to:

First	3s 2d (16p)
Second	2s 8d (14p)
Third	1s 11½d (10p)

The branch was always worked by the NER, and the 1858 timetable suggests that the last train to Kelso formed the first train next day back to Berwick. Possibly the train was stabled at Kelso until the engine shed at Sprouston was built in 1863, when the empty stock worked back there each night. The normal journey time for the 23½ miles from Berwick to Kelso was one hour and ten minutes; the fastest being about 50 minutes when stops between Coldstream and Kelso were omitted. Surprisingly, the potential for through passenger trains between Berwick and St Boswells was virtually ignored during the branches' lifetime, with long waits for connections being usual at Kelso.

When the Alnwick to Coldstream (A&C) opened in 1887 the weekday service increased from Coldstream to Berwick by one train, but, as there was no Sunday service on the new branch, Sunday trains remained at two.[14] The passengers served by the A&C soon agitated for market trains to run on Saturday afternoons, and the one from Alnwick ran through to Berwick, but the one in the opposite direction connected with existing services at Coldstream. On alternate Mondays, to coincide with the Wooler livestock marts, an autocar service left Kelso around 8.00 am for Wooler and returned empty stock to Tweedmouth.

The peak weekday service on the line, of six trains a day, commenced about 1900, but after the outset of the First World War the number was reduced to four. Bradshaw's timetable for 1922 shows three trains throughout the branch in each direction, and there were two trains each way serving the A&C with an additional morning train from Coldstream to Berwick. The Sunday service remained at two trains.

The A&C closed to passengers in September 1930, but the service to Kelso remained at four trains a day, with an additional return train during August. Through running from St Boswells to Berwick was introduced on one train each way. From 1932 until 1941 some trains were 'one class only' suggesting that the six-cylinder Sentinel steam railcar *Royal Charlotte*, which was stationed at Tweedmouth, was being used.[15] The summer Sunday timetable from 1937 to 1939 gave only one train and it ran through between Newcastle and Edinburgh stopping only at Norham and

Coldstream in each direction; the Sunday service ceased altogether at the outbreak of the Second World War. The wartime and immediate post-war timetable saw three trains throughout in each direction plus a return morning service from Berwick to Coldstream. Oddly, during this period, the early afternoon train to Berwick started its journey at Jedburgh, but there was no reverse working.[16]

The opening of the Border Union Railway between Hawick and Carlisle in 1862, and Berwickshire Railway, from St Boswells to Reston via Duns in 1863, removed the Kelso lines' monopoly for traffic to the east and the south of the main Border towns. Soon there were regular through services between Berwick and St Boswells, via Reston and Duns, taking little more than $1^1/_2$ hours. The wait for connections on most trains via Kelso meant far longer overall times. Oddly, the wait was blamed on having to connect with main line services at each end, but, true or not, it did not help to attract potential passengers to the line.

The introduction of local bus services, the growth of road transport and car ownership meant that closures of stations became inevitable. On 7 December 1953 Twizell became an unstaffed halt and public delivery siding, and on 4 July 1955 all the stations except Norham and Coldstream were closed to passengers. These two survived for another nine years until 15 June 1964 with the final timetable providing only two trains each way between Berwick and St Boswells. With an average of only six passengers per train the route was losing nearly £58,000 per annum prior to closure.[17] The goods facilities were removed between 1960 and 29 March 1965.

Although the branch was rarely used for timetabled services to Edinburgh it was available as part of a diversion if the main line north of Berwick was blocked. Trains then ran via St Boswells and the Waverley Route, as the alternative via the Newcastle & Carlisle and the WCML was much longer. For two-and-a-half months in 1948 the line gained fame as part of the East Coast route to Edinburgh. On 12 August 1948 prolonged torrential rainfall fell on already saturated ground on the Lammermuir Hills and the area to the south-east of them. The scale of the downpour was such that the rivers and streams were totally inadequate to cope and damage to property, roads and railways was extreme. Seven bridges on the ECML between Berwick and Dunbar were destroyed, and the A&C, Berwickshire, Eyemouth and Jedburgh branches also lost structures. There were a number of landslides between Edinburgh and St Boswells and the Kelso line suffered one between Sprouston and Carham; amazingly, all were cleared to allow the diversion to be used *within four days* of the inundation. The diversion, which was $15^3/_4$ miles longer than the main line, was not ideal for running passenger trains loaded up to 500 tons, and the schedule had to be increased by 90 minutes (this was later reduced by about 25 minutes). From Edinburgh to Falahill summit it required a climb of 700 feet, including ten miles of gradients averaging 1 in 75. The line between St Boswells and Kelso had been singled in 1933, and

local passenger services were temporarily withdrawn over this section to give the maximum number of paths for the diverted services; main-line locomotives were restricted to 35 rather than the normal 45 mph from St Boswells to Tweedmouth. While the engineers worked wonders in reinstating the main line, the operating staff and enginemen provided an outstanding service in very difficult circumstances. On no less than 23 occasions the *Flying Scotsman* was able to make its scheduled, summer, non-stop run between the two capitals – a distance of nearly 409 miles. The main line was opened with temporary bridges by the end of October, but weekend diversions were needed for the next year to allow the permanent structures to be built.[18]

In the headlong rush to close railways after the Beeching Report in 1963, a lesson that could have been learned from the diversions was the possibility of just closing the Waverley Route south of Hawick but retaining the line from St Boswells to Tweedmouth. This was never considered even when equally loss-making lines in more sparsely populated areas of the Scottish Highlands were allowed to retain their railways. The mistake of closing all railways in the Borders between the ECML and WCML has now been realised with the expensive reinstatement of the Waverley Route between Edinburgh and Galashiels being a firm proposal.[19]

Endnotes:

1. This chapter is condensed from a longer article by the author, which appeared in the *North Eastern Express, Volume 42, No 171,* September 2003, pages 64 - 75.

2. Professor Sir Alec Skempton (editor) *Biographical Dictionary of Civil Engineers Volume 1,* (2002) pages 565, 694. In 1810 Thomas Telford produced a report and plans for an iron-railway from Glasgow to Berwick via the Tweed Valley.

3. Deposited Plans, Northumberland County Record Office.

4. *Ibid.*

5. N&B Minutes.

6. NER Line Diagrams, NERA Collection.

7. The National Archives MT6 5/110.

8. J & B Green's statement of contracts and payments for the buildings on N&B.

9. *LNER Station Traffic Index 1925*: Section A.

10. Hoole, K. *North Eastern Locomotive Sheds* (1972) page 215.

11. Teasdale, JG (Editor) *Servicing the North Eastern Railway's Locomotives,* (2007) pages 24, 32 and 52. Drawings of Coldstream turntable appear on pages 58 and 59.

12. Foster, CB (Editor) *North Eastern Record, Volume 1,* (1988) pages 73 - 7, gives signal box types.

13. Maclean, AA. *LNER Constituent Signalling,* (1983) page 216 gives a drawing of Velvet Hall signal box.

14. Addyman, JF and Mallon, JF. *The Alnwick and Cornhill Railway,* (2007) pages 63 - 4.

15. *Locomotives of the LNER, Part 10B,* (1990) page 46.

16. Specimen railway timetables between 1849 and 1964.

17. Mullay, AJ. *Rails Across the Border*, (1990), page 46.

18. Dow, G. *Railway World* (September – November 1968) 'Deluge over the Border'.

19. The Act to reinstate the line was given Royal Assent in July 2006; the estimated costs had escalated to over £200 million by the time that the first sod was cut at Galashiels on 3 March 2010.

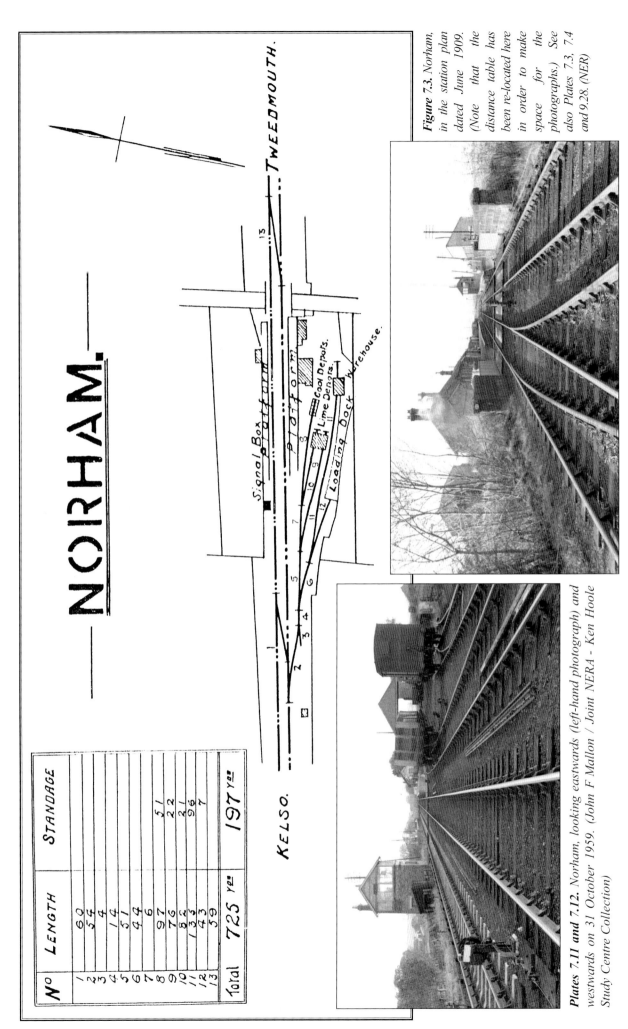

NORHAM.

Nᵒ	LENGTH	STANDAGE
1	60	
2	54	
3	4	
4	14	
5	51	
6	44	
7	6	
8	97	51
9	76	22
10	85	21
11	133	96
12	43	7
13	59	
Total	725 ʸᴰˢ	197 ʸᴰˢ

KELSO.

TWEEDMOUTH.

Signal Box

Station

Platform

Coal Depots.

Lime Depots.

Loading Dock

Warehouse.

Figure 7.3. Norham, in the station plan dated June 1909. (Note that the distance table has been re-located here in order to make space for the photographs.) See also Plates 7.3, 7.4 and 9.28. (NER)

Plates 7.11 and 7.12. Norham, looking eastwards (left-hand photograph) and westwards on 31 October 1959. (John F Mallon / Joint NERA - Ken Hoole Study Centre Collection)

Chapter 8 : Signalling between Newcastle and Berwick

Neil Mackay

The earliest forms of signalling employed on the Newcastle & Berwick Railway would have been similar to other contemporary railways – stations would have had some form of semaphore or disc signal which would have been used to stop a train or to indicate that it could proceed. Working would be by timetable, or by time interval between trains proceeding in the same direction. At level crossings a simple hut would provide shelter for the keeper.

The report on the collision at Red Barns Siding (Ouseburn) on 30 June 1871 [1] gives a good picture of the relatively simple signalling employed prior to introduction of the block system and interlocking. An Up Scotch Express (10.20 am ex Edinburgh) collided with an engine and two coal wagons. The engine had been shunting when the signalman told the driver to clear the Down Main for a train which was waiting to pass. Owing to a misunderstanding the driver brought his engine through the crossover road – which, like the siding points, was not worked from the cabin and not interlocked with the signals – to the Up Main. At this moment the Up express appeared from Heaton (under clear signals as the signalman had not noticed the position of the engine and wagons) and despite emergency braking a collision took place. Captain Tyler remarked that the cabin 'contains a good clock' which was a prerequisite of timetable working. The Up and Down home signals were on one post close to the cabin; the Down distant was 410 yards from the home, and the Up distant was 495 yards away.

By the early 1870s the NER – under pressure from the Board of Trade – had come to realise that it was necessary to adopt the block telegraph system. Mr A Christison (the NER General Passenger Superintendent) made a survey of the company's lines to determine the amount of work needed and fortunately his reports survive. The Newcastle to Berwick report [2] is dated 16 January 1873 and there were only a few structures deemed suitable for the new system. The buildings were mainly too small or in the wrong location: at Beal mention is made of '...the existing gate cabin which is too small for block working.' However, some buildings were just acceptable – at Berwick there was a '...permanent ground cabin west of the lines...' which was '...rather small but will do for what block working is required.' In the Newcastle area, some cabins were already being erected or had just been completed. At Cramlington the platform frame '...only requires a suitable cabin built over it.'

No fewer than 22 new signal cabins were proposed and it appears that all of them were actually constructed. These were in general to the style later classified as N1;[3] particularly north of Alnmouth they were built of stone, brick being used further south. As was usual at this time, the NER invited bids for the signal equipment and a variety of manufacturers supplied lever frames and outdoor apparatus.

In conformance with general NER practice, the lever frames were installed nearest to the running line, so that the signalman faced the lines when operating the levers.

The signals themselves were generally of wooden construction, with a slotted post but frequently fitted with a ball-and-spike finial, as was common throughout the Northern Division. In the early days of the block system they showed a red light at night for 'stop', and white for 'all clear'. It was not until the 1890s that green began to replace white. Facing connections were very rare and trailing points were not detected by the signals, an 'indicator' (usually a short-armed semaphore) being worked by the same lever.

Traffic growth in the 1890s was matched by improvements in the signalling system. In the Newcastle area much new work was undertaken in 1893, only to be replaced after 16 years by an electro-pneumatic installation which at the time was the very latest technology. Line capacity further north was restricted by the need to shunt slower-moving freight trains to allow overtaking by passenger trains. In 1900 this was addressed between Chevington and Amble Junction where new Up and Down Independents were provided together with a new signal box – a 'bridge cabin' built over the main running lines – at Amble Junction. In 1901 a new signal cabin was built at Goswick along with a new Up Independent to Beal. As the independent lines were used for freight traffic only, they were controlled using permissive block ('recording block' in NER parlance) so that more than one train could occupy the section. The new installations were noticeably more complex than those dating from the 1870s, with multiple miniature semaphores for shunting moves, detection of trailing points, and a corresponding increase in the size of lever frame.

Resignalling Schemes

By the end of the 19th Century the physical equipment at the major centres was becoming life-expired after some 30 years of service, and the track layouts from the 1870s were unable to provide sufficient flexibility. Major resignalling schemes were undertaken at Belford (1901), Tweedmouth (1902), Morpeth and Alnmouth (1907), and Benton Bank (1908); additionally, there were numerous other improvements such as the work at Chathill in 1911.

During and immediately after the First World War further traffic growth put pressure on the line capacity and the opportunity was taken to install more independents. The first of these was a new Down Independent from Beal to Goswick in 1918, followed in 1920-21 by Dudley Colliery to Dam Dykes, Stannington to Clifton Crossing, Wooden Gate to Alnmouth and Little Mill to Stamford Crossing. Finally in 1925 came Belford to Crag Mill. In all cases from 1920 an existing gate cabin at one end of the independents was replaced by a new signal cabin. This avoided a net increase in manpower, though higher wages were paid. The new cabins were fitted with McKenzie & Holland No16 pattern lever frames, which had become the company standard for new works and replacements.

During the spring of 1928, the red spectacle plates and arms which had, up to that time, been used at distant signals were replaced by yellow glasses and arms showing a chevron stripe. The crews worked from south to north, and had completed the work as far as Berwick by mid-May.

In the early 1930s work began on improving the sighting of signals – perhaps in anticipation of higher speed services – and an unusual solution was adopted. This involved removing the semaphore arms and replacing the oil lamp with a more powerful electric version which was visible in daylight. Sometimes a round target was fitted in front of the spectacle plate, giving a similar overall appearance to a conventional colour-light signal. The advantage over full conversion

to colour lights was an economic one – few, if any, changes in interlocking were needed, though cabling was required for the lights as well as bulb filament repeaters. The use of these signals was to become quite widespread (see tables in Appendix 3A), and extended to other locations on the ECML further south.

By the mid-1950s much of the signalling equipment was well over 50 years old and was worn out. At the same time the new British Railways Modernisation Plan envisaged spending £100 million on signalling improvements.[4] The North Eastern Region was keen to spend some of this on the Newcastle to Berwick main line, and approval was obtained for a large relay interlocking at Newcastle, replacing the 1909 electro-pneumatic signalling. A 'low budget' conversion of the main line north to Berwick was devised, with smaller relay interlocking schemes at Heaton, Benton, Belford and Tweedmouth (referred to as the 'Heaton to Burnmouth Resignalling'),

Plate 8.1. *The second signal cabin at Belford was opened around 1901 and is seen here towards the end of its life. (See also Colour Plate 10 on page 40). This is a typical NER Northern Division 'bridge cabin' and this version spans three lines – the Down Main, Up Main, and dock (reading left to right). The cabin is of timber carried on lattice girders; these buildings were susceptible to locomotive sparks and several were destroyed in fires started this way. Smoke troughs have been fitted over the Up Main and dock to help in containing the sparks. The main Up home signal (No 48 in the original frame, later No 20) and shunting signal from the Down to the Up Main, or to the Down Relief Siding (No 47, later No 37) were attached to the structure and can be seen at the far side. The gates were extra long as the lines to the goods yard also crossed the road to the right (off the photograph). The N&B goods shed can be seen beyond the cabin. In the left distance the junction signals for the Down Independent to Crag Mill can just be made out. (BR (NER), collection of Chris Woolstenholmes)*

and contracts were awarded to Westinghouse Brake and Signal Company. The Newcastle scheme involved the closure of Nos 1, 2 and 3 boxes along with Manors; a new signal box and relay room was built over Platform 10 at the Central Station. The control area was subsequently extended towards Heaton; the new relay interlocking here was situated along the Tynemouth lines but controlled the main line as far as Benton. The fact that yet another relay interlocking was provided barely two miles further down the line at Benton Quarry is hard to understand, as it could easily have been incorporated into the Heaton scheme.

Beyond Benton, it was decided to retain most of the signal cabins and, in general, their mechanical lever frames. This decision was most probably influenced by the large number of level crossings; automatic barriers were still in their infancy, so that a gatekeeper was required anyway, and he could also operate the signals. Where possible, block posts were reduced to gate cabins released remotely. Where independents were provided, control was concentrated at one end, with the remote end cabin being reduced to gate cabin status, released from the controlling cabin. Four-aspect colour light signals with full track circuiting were provided in place of the semaphores (and the mechanical colour lights) to allow faster running and increase braking distances. Track circuit block replaced the absolute block system and, in keeping with the route's status, the Automatic Warning System (AWS) was in most cases installed at the same time. At several locations new mechanical frames were provided; where this was done, the new frame was generally furthest away from the lines so that the signalman had his back to traffic when operating the levers. (As a consequence the open fire was replaced by a cast-iron stove, located towards the front of the building).

At Belford and Tweedmouth, entirely new structures were provided. These followed contemporary architectural practice with a glazed 'control tower' atop one end of the relay room; their wide flat roof and sloped windows (both to counter glare) gave them a pleasing and distinctive appearance. That at Tweedmouth still survives, as does the relay room at Belford.

During the late 1960s changing traffic patterns and the search for cost savings brought about the closure of the independents from Dudley to Dam Dykes (1968), Stannington to Clifton Crossing (1967), Little Mill to Stamford Crossing (1967), and Beal to Goswick (1966).

In the mid 1970s plans were made to introduce high-speed diesel trains to the ECML and it was decided to make further improvements to the signalling between Newcastle and Berwick. This involved converting numerous manned level crossings to lifting barriers supervised by another signal cabin using closed circuit television. At the same time, signal spacing was adjusted where necessary to provide suitable braking distances for the new trains. The signalling was controlled from only eight locations: Benton, Stannington, Morpeth (where a new cabin was built), Chevington, Alnmouth, Chathill, Belford and Tweedmouth.

Further rationalisation took place in the early 1990s resulting in the closure of Benton, Stannington, Chevington, Chathill and Belford. At the same time, the opportunity was taken to introduce full bi-directional working on certain sections; this had previously only been seen in the immediate vicinity of Newcastle. A simplified bi-directional working facility was provided for much of the route; this is intended for emergency use and engineering possessions. At the time of writing the Newcastle - Berwick railway is controlled by Tyneside IECC, Morpeth, Alnmouth and Tweedmouth only – a far cry from the 55 block posts shown in the 1922 WTT Appendix.

As usual the accidents on the line were caused by human error, mechanical failures, track defects and weather and are amply summarized by JA Wells in *Signals to Danger : Railway Accidents at Newcastle upon Tyne and in Northumberland 1851-1992* (1992).

Plate 8.2. Benton Quarry cabin is seen after a fall of snow. This is the second cabin at this location and dates from 1903; the new west curve to Benton station opening that year, followed by the east curve in 1904. The original cabin was at the top of the cutting; this one is a style N2 building. It was replaced after just over 60 years by Benton PSB located on the opposite side of the lines. Note the conductor rails in the foreground, also dating from the same period as the building. (BR (NER), collection of Chris Woolstenholmes)

Acknowledgements:
Richard Pulleyn, John Midcalf, Peter Hawes, Michael Rising, Ken Appleby, John Whitaker and Nicholas Fleetwood gave much assistance in the compilation of these notes, and were instrumental in compiling the comprehensive Appendix 3. The collections of the late John Boyes, Chris Woolstenholmes, John Mallon and John Talbot were invaluable sources of information, together with the Railway Inspectorate reports held by the National Archives.

Endnotes:
1. Report by Captain HW Tyler, 7 August 1871, available at http://www.railwaysarchive.co.uk/documents/BoT_RedBarnsSidings1971.pdf
2. *Memorandum of Proposed Block Signalling Stations between Newcastle and Berwick*, York, 1873. National Archives RAIL527/1117.
3. Foster, CB (Editor) *North Eastern Record Volume 1*, 1988, pages 73-7.
4. *Modernisation & Improvement of British Railways*, BTC, London, 1955, pages 10-11.

Plate 8.3. Dudley Colliery (formerly Annitsford Colliery Junction) is a rather uninspiring style N1 brick building typical of those south of Morpeth and dating from the mid 1870s. It has been extended at the north end, as seen by the change in brickwork, to accommodate a larger lever frame required when the Up and Down Independents to Dam Dykes were opened in 1920. As part of the 1962 re-signalling, control was extended to Dam Dykes and to accommodate the necessary relays, a further single-storey extension was made. A former station lamp (note the slot for a name tablet) serves to illuminate the Down wicket gate. Some of the windows were later replaced with a domestic design and the remaining spaces boarded over, which did nothing to improve the aesthetic appeal of the building. (BR (NER), collection of Chris Woolstenholmes)

Plate 8.4. Stamford Crossing is a style N4 cabin erected in 1920 in conjunction with the opening of the Up and Down Independents from Little Mill. It is not clear why such a large box was required; there were several spares in the 31-lever frame. Mechanical barriers worked by the gate wheel were installed in 1965. The building was demolished upon closure and the outhouses (seen to the right) were converted into a relay room. (Chris Woolstenholmes)

Plate 8.5. *A good impression of the Heaton to Burnmouth resignalling is conveyed by this official view at the north end of the Dudley Colliery to Dam Dykes loops. Four-aspect Down Main signal DC16 is suspended on the lightweight tubular lattice to give good sighting and keep the six-foot clear. A telephone box at lower level allows the train crew to contact the signalman. On the Down Loop, DC15 is a conventional 3-aspect signal controlling the outlet to the Down Main. Two steel location cabinets (267a and 267b) and concrete cable troughs are seen to the left. Dam Dykes cabin – no longer a block post by this time – is visible in the distance. (BR (NER), collection of Chris Woolstenholmes)*

Plate 8.6. *Chevington is a style N2 stone building dating from 1899. It was subsequently extended at the south end as can be seen from the lighter-coloured stones and (now) off-centre locking room windows. The photograph, looking south, was taken on 26 October 1959. After closure of the signal box, the base was converted to a relay room. (John F Mallon / Joint NERA / Ken Hoole Study Centre John Mallon Collection)*

Plate 8.7. Alnmouth North is seen just after resignalling in 1907. This was a large scheme and involved the construction of two new signal cabins along with a large number of lattice post signals and steel gantries supplied by McKenzie & Holland of Worcester. Most, if not all, possible moves were covered by fixed signals, and learning the application of each arm presented a challenge to locomotive crews. To assist with this it seems that the arms of the shunting signals were labelled – see the arm on the very far right. This applied to movements from the gas works siding and was worked by lever 82 in the 116 lever frame. As best as can be deduced this arm was lettered FROM GAS WORKS SIDING. It is not known how the lettering was applied – perhaps a paper label which would become detached after a time. The smaller arms on the gantry also appear to be lettered; the main arm (No 104, INDEPENDENT TO UP SIGNAL) was not. Many of the gantries survived until the end of semaphore signalling in 1964; Alnmouth North cabin is still in use today. (Joint NERA / Ken Hoole Study Centre John Mallon Collection)

Plate 8.8. The photograph, taken on 4 March 1953, shows the very tall signal needed at Alnmouth North to allow adequate sighting distance for Down trains beyond the overbridge at the south end of the station. Note the lower quadrant signal at the top of the post, but the more modern co-acting upper quadrant signal at the bottom. (John RP Bennett)

Chapter 9 : Train Services

John F Addyman

Passenger Trains

The Newcastle & Berwick was never a particularly busy main line, but, with the recent upsurge in rail travel, it now has twice as many passenger trains than ever before. The speeds for the faster trains, throughout the first half of its life, though not fast, were comparable with those on other main lines, and exceeded the Victorian standard of the 40 mph average needed for them to qualify as expresses. Rivalry between the East and West-Coast companies, resulted in races in 1888 and 1895, showed that much higher speeds were possible with lightweight trains, but these were certainly not commercially viable and nothing of value accrued to the travelling public. In fact, an agreement following the races resulted in a minimum schedule of $8^1/_4$ hours being imposed between King's Cross and Edinburgh; it was not lifted until 1932.

With the first two parts of the line between Newcastle (Carliol Square) and Morpeth and Chathill to Tweedmouth being opened on 5 April 1847, a service using four trains over each section connected with coach services, involving three changes, to get from

YORK, NEWCASTLE, & BERWICK RAILWAY.

STATIONS.	DOWN TRAINS FROM YORK TO BERWICK.											SUNDAYS.								FARES.			
	1	2	3	4	5	6	7	8	9		10	11	12	13	14	15	16	17	18	1st clas	2nd clas	3rd clas	4th clas
	1 2 3 A.M.	A.M.		1 2 3 A.M.	1 2 P.M.	P.M.	1 2 3 P.M.				P.M.	1 2 3 A.M.		A.M.		1 2 3 P.M			P. M.				
Newcastle	7 0	9 30	....	1 30	3 45	6 20	6 45	....	....	....	11 30	7 15	....	9 30	....	6 5	....	....	11 30	....	....	....	....
Killingworth	7 12	....	....	1 43	3 51	....	6 58	....	....	....	....	7 27	....	....	....	6 18	....	....	....	1 3	0 9	....	0 5¼
Cramlington	7 21	....	....	1 52	4 2	....	7 7	....	....	....	....	7 37	....	....	....	6 27	....	....	....	1 9	1 3	....	0 9¾
Netherton	7 30	....	....	2 2	4 12	....	7 17	....	....	....	....	7 47	....	....	....	6 37	....	....	....	2 6	1 9	....	1 1¾
Morpeth	7 38	10 5	....	2 11	4 21	6 45	7 26	....	....	....	....	7 55	....	10 5	....	6 46	....	....	....	3 0	2 0	....	1 4½
Longhirst	7 45	....	....	2 18	4 34	....	7 33	....	....	....	....	8 4	....	....	....	6 54	....	....	....	4 0	2 6	....	1 8
Widdrington	7 58	....	....	2 32	4 42	....	7 47	....	....	....	....	8 12	....	....	....	7 7	....	....	....	5 0	3 0	....	1 11
Acklington	8 10	10 30	....	2 44	4 54	....	7 59	....	....	....	....	8 25	....	10 30	....	7 21	....	....	....	6 0	3 9	....	2 4¼
Warkworth	8 18	....	....	2 53	5 5	....	8 8	....	....	....	....	8 31	....	....	....	7 28	....	....	....	6 6	4 0	....	2 6¾
Lesbury, Alnwick	8 29	10 45	....	3 4	5 14	7 10	8 19	....	....	....	....	8 41	....	10 45	....	7 39	....	....	....	7 6	4 6	....	2 10¾
Longhoughton	8 35	....	....	3 11	5 21	....	8 26	....	....	....	....	8 47	....	....	....	7 46	....	....	....	8 0	5 0	....	3 1¼
Christon Bank	8 49	....	....	3 26	5 36	....	8 41	....	....	....	....	9 4	....	....	....	8 1	....	....	....	9 0	5 6	....	3 6¾
Chat-hill	8 57	....	....	3 34	5 44	....	3 49	....	....	....	....	9 8	....	....	....	8 9	....	....	....	9 6	6 0	....	3 9¾
Lucker	9 5	....	....	3 43	5 53	....	8 58	....	....	....	....	9 16	....	....	....	8 18	....	....	....	10 0	6 3	....	4 1
Belford	9 10	11 15	....	3 48	5 59	....	9 3	....	....	....	....	9 22	....	11 15	....	8 23	....	....	....	10 9	6 6	....	4 3¼
Beal	9 26	....	....	4 5	6 18	....	9 20	....	....	....	....	9 40	....	....	....	8 40	....	....	....	12 0	7 6	....	4 10¼
Scremerston	9 35	....	....	4 15	6 30	....	9 30	....	....	....	....	9 50	....	....	....	8 50	....	....	....	13 0	8 0	....	5 3¼
Tweedmouth	9 43	11 43	....	4 23	6 38	....	9 38	....	....	....	....	9 58	....	11 43	....	8 58	....	....	....	13 6	8 6	....	5 5½
ARRIVE AT											A.M.								A.M.				
Berwick	9 45	11 45	....	4 25	6 40	8 5	9 40	....	....	....	2 0	10 0	....	11 45	....	9 0	....	....	2 0	14 0	8 9	....	5 7½
	P.M.	P.M.												P.M.									
Edinburgh	12 5	2 5	....	7 0	9 40	9 40	....	....	....	....	5 15	....	....	2 5	....	....	....	....	5 15	....	....	....	....
Glasgow	2 30	4 15	....	....	11 20	11 20	....	....	....	....	....	....	....	....	....	....	....	....	....	....	....	....	....

DURHAM.—Passengers can book at Durham for London (and places South of York at which the Up Express stops) by a Special Train leaving at 1 25 p.m.—The Down Express will stop at Belmont with Passengers from London and places South of York.

YORK, NEWCASTLE, & BERWICK RAILWAY.

STATIONS.	UP TRAINS FROM BERWICK TO YORK.											SUNDAYS.								FARES.			
	1	2	3	4	5	6	7	8	9		10	11	12	13	14	15	16	17	18	1st clas	2nd clas	3rd clas	4th Class
				Expr:		Mail					Mail				Mail				Mail				1d.m.
LEAVE			A.M.	a.m.	a.m.	a. m.			p.m.		p.m.			a.m.	a.m.			p.m.	p.m.	s. d.	s. d.	s. d.	s. d.
Glasgow	....	....	....	8 0	....	....	....	....	....	....	4 0	....	....	....	....	....	....	....	....	....	....	....	....
Edinburgh	....	....	....	9 45	8 0	11 0	....	....	....	....	6 0	....	....	....	11 0	....	....	....	6 0	....	....	....	....
			1 2 3 Cl a.m.	1 Class a.m.	1 2 3 Class a.m.	1 2 Class a.m.			1 2 3 Cl p.m.		1 2 Class p.m.			1 2 3 Class a.m.	1 2 Class p.m.			1 2 3 Cl p.m.	1 2 Class p.m.				
Berwick	....	....	7 15	11 20	10 45	1 15	....	....	5 30	....	8 35	....	....	7 0	1 15	....	....	5 15	8 35	....	....	....	....
Tweedmouth	....	....	7 17	....	10 47	1 17	....	....	5 32	....	8 37	....	....	7 2	1 17	....	....	5 17	8 37	0 6	0 3	....	0 2
Scremerston	....	....	7 22	....	10 52	....	....	....	5 37	....	....	....	....	7 7	....	....	....	5 22	....	1 0	0 8	....	0 6
Beal	....	....	7 32	....	11 2	....	....	....	5 47	....	....	....	....	7 17	....	....	....	5 32	....	1 9	1 3	....	0 9¼
Belford	....	....	7 48	....	11 18	1 43	....	....	6 3	....	9 2	....	....	7 34	1 43	....	....	5 49	9 2	3 6	2 0	....	1 4¼
Lucker	....	....	7 55	....	11 25	....	....	....	6 8	....	....	....	....	7 41	....	....	....	5 56	....	4 0	2 6	....	1 6½
Chat Hill	....	....	8 2	....	11 32	....	....	....	6 15	....	....	....	....	7 48	....	....	....	6 3	....	4 6	2 9	....	1 9¾
Christon Bank	....	....	8 7	....	11 37	....	....	....	6 21	....	....	....	....	7 54	....	....	....	6 10	....	5 0	3 3	....	2 0¾
Longhoughton	....	....	8 24	....	11 54	....	....	....	6 36	....	....	....	....	8 11	....	....	....	6 27	....	6 6	3 9	....	2 6¼
Lesbury, Alnwick	....	....	8 29	11 55	11 59	2 15	....	....	6 42	....	9 32	....	....	8 17	2 15	....	....	6 33	9 32	7 0	4 3	....	2 8¾
Warkworth	....	....	8 42	....	12 12	....	....	....	6 54	....	....	....	....	8 30	....	....	....	6 46	....	7 6	4 9	....	3 0¾
Acklington	....	....	8 52	....	12 21	2 30	....	....	7 4	....	9 47	....	....	8 40	2 30	....	....	6 56	9 47	8 6	5 0	....	3 3¼
Widdrington	....	....	9 3	....	12 33	....	....	....	7 14	....	....	....	....	8 52	....	....	....	7 8	....	9 6	5 9	....	3 8½
Longhirst	....	....	9 11	....	12 41	....	....	....	7 23	....	....	....	....	9 0	....	....	....	7 16	....	10 0	6 3	....	3 11½
Morpeth	....	....	9 19	12 25	12 49	2 55	....	....	7 33	....	10 10	....	....	9 9	2 55	....	....	7 25	10 10	11 0	6 9	....	4 3
Netherton	....	....	9 28	....	12 58	....	....	....	7 43	....	....	....	....	9 18	....	....	....	7 34	....	11 6	6 9	....	4 5¾
Cramlington	....	....	9 40	....	1 10	....	....	....	7 53	....	....	....	....	9 30	....	....	....	7 46	....	12 0	7 3	....	4 9¾
Killingworth	....	....	9 50	....	1 20	....	....	....	8 2	....	....	....	....	9 41	....	....	....	7 57	....	13 0	7 9	....	5 2
ARRIVE AT										....	....	....	....										
Newcastle	....	....	10 15	1 5	1 45	3 30	....	....	8 15	....	....	....	....	10 0	3 30	....	....	8 15	10 45	14 0	8 9	....	5 7½

__Figure 9.1.__ Part of Reid's timetable for April 1849 showing the passenger services on the Newcastle & Berwick. The classes of passengers carried by each train are given at the top of the columns, and the fares are on the right-hand side. Note that Third and Fourth (Parliamentary) Class are both charged at one penny per mile. The fares are charged to and from Newcastle Carliol Square (Manors).

Newcastle to Berwick. Three months later, from 1 July, six trains in each direction ran through from Newcastle to Tweedmouth, but it was to be more than 15 months before they could run over the temporary Tweed viaduct into Berwick. The April 1849 timetable gave the fastest train, carrying First Class passengers only, taking one-and-three-quarter hours and the 'Parliamentary trains', stopping at all stations, under three hours. (Figure 9.1)

In November 1855 an agreement was reached between the Great Northern, North Eastern and North British Railways for 'establishing a united system of facilitating the transit of traffic' along the ECML, and 1861 saw the first purpose-built trains of 'East Coast Joint Stock' in use.[1] On the Newcastle & Berwick, in the same year, the 'all stations' and the fastest trains, now carrying Second Class passengers, showed no improvement at all in speed, but the frequency had increased to seven in each direction with additional 'market day' trains running over parts of the line on Saturdays. The introduction of block-signalling and continuous brakes during the 1870s was followed by significant increases in speed. In the 1880s the number of trains had doubled, and the best was 20 minutes faster than when the line was completed in 1850. By the end of the NER's independence, in January 1923, there had been little improvement to the faster schedules, and the 'all stations' were still taking around three hours.

The races between London and Edinburgh in 1888 and London and Aberdeen in 1895 produced some very spectacular times; the best, in August 1895, from Euston to Aberdeen were 512 minutes for the 540 miles (63.2 mph), and from King's Cross to Aberdeen 520 minutes for the 523 miles (60.6 mph). On 21 August Newcastle to Edinburgh saw some of the fastest running of the races; Berwick, 66.9 miles from Newcastle, was passed in exactly one hour, and

Edinburgh, 124.4 miles, was reached in 113 minutes – 7 minutes faster than the 'Coronation' service introduced 42 years later. Over the 104.2 miles from Longhirst, north of Morpeth, to Edinburgh the average speed was 68.14 mph, the highest to be achieved over a distance in excess of 100 miles by any of the contestants. Worsdell class M1 4-4-0 No 1620, driver Bob Nicholson and fireman Tom Blades were responsible for this outstanding performance.[2]

Such times between Newcastle and Edinburgh were only possible because it was not necessary to change the NER for NBR locomotives at the Berwick frontier. An agreement of 1862 had allowed NBR trains to run over the NER between Hexham and Newcastle, and the NER to haul through passenger trains over the NBR between Berwick and Edinburgh. The NER did not start to use its powers until June 1869, but it gradually ousted the NBR from running any expresses over its own main line. In 1871 the NBR seemed agreeable to the arrangement and even completed a shed at St Margaret's, Edinburgh, to be rented to the NER who, at busy times, stabled more than 12 locomotives there.[3] However, relations between the two companies became more and more acrimonious, resulting in litigation and eventually, in January 1897, the NBR taking over the working of all trains between Berwick and Edinburgh by their own locomotives. A judgement by the Railway and Canal Commissioner (Scotland), in 1898, divided the services between the two companies, but in 1904 the NBR agreed that the NER could again work all the through trains.[4]

A number of famous trains were to travel over the line; some like the 'Coronation' streamliner were short lived (1937-39), but one has survived for nearly 150 years. In 1862 the 'Scotch Express', later known as the 'Flying Scotsman', started to leave London and Edinburgh simultaneously at 10-0 am. Acceleration in

Plate 9.1. *The NER started installing water troughs at Lucker in 1896, immediately after the race to Aberdeen. They were brought into use on 1 March 1898 for East-Coast trains not timed to stop at Berwick. (JC Dean, circa 1962)*

1872 reduced the journey time by one hour to 9 hours 5 minutes, including a 25 minute lunch stop at York. In July 1893 the first bogie vehicles, dining cars, were introduced on expresses leaving Edinburgh and King's Cross at 2-30 pm, but it was not until 1900 that they were included in the 'Flying Scotsman', allowing the lunch stop at York to be eliminated. Complete trains of bogie vehicles were introduced in 1895, and the extra accommodation and facilities provided for passengers increased the weight of a typical train by almost a third over that of the previous four and six-wheeled stock.[1] Immediately before Grouping, the heavy 'Flying Scotsman' was allowed 83 minutes to cover the 67 miles from Newcastle (48mph), before pausing for 5 minutes in Berwick; the total time from King's Cross to Edinburgh was 8½ hours.

On 1 May 1928 the 'Flying Scotsman' commenced its world record, non-stop run between the capitals, initially taking the agreed 8 ¼ hours for the 393-mile journey (47.6 mph). A pact between the LNER and LMSR allowed its timings to be reduced in 1932 to 7½ hours and further reduced in 1937 to 7 hours (56.1 mph).[5] Figure 9.2 shows the timetable for Down passenger trains in the summer of 1939. The Second World War not only brought the end of non-stop running but the introduction of much reduced speeds, which were in force for more than a decade. The 1946 summer timetable saw the 'Flying Scotsman' taking 8 hours 18 minutes over its journey, which including a three-minute stop at Berwick. The floods of August 1948 added 90 minutes for the diversions, and with severe speed restrictions still needed when the line re-opened north of Berwick, the 1949 timetable allowed the 'Flying Scotsman' 8 hours 28 minutes (46.1 mph).

Main-line diesels appeared on the railway in 1957, and the first 3,300 hp 'Deltic' ran in 1961; the Deltics were able to equal the pre-war 'Coronation' schedule of 6 hours (65.5 mph). The Deltics continued to reign for almost two decades until the full High Speed Train (HST) or 'Inter City 125' service was introduced on 20 August 1979, allowing the reduction of the total time to less than 5 hours; Newcastle to Berwick typically took 47 minutes. The fastest 2010 East-Coast electric service takes 4 hours 13 minutes (93.2 mph) between the capitals – half the 1949 time. A demonstration run, on 26 September 1991, following the completion of the ECML electrification, gave the fastest ever time of 3 hours 29 minutes (112.8 mph). The average of 106 mph between Newcastle and Berwick was a lot slower than that which could have been achieved if Lord Grey had not objected to the original Stephenson alignment. At the time of writing, East Coast and Cross Country services stopping at Berwick take between 41 and 43 minutes from Newcastle.

For most of the railway's life an average 15 through trains per day ran in each direction, with around eight additional stopping trains between either

Table 157.   NEWCASTLE, MORPETH, ALNMOUTH, BERWICK, DUNBAR AND EDINBURGH.

WEEKDAYS

	Table	pm	pm	pm	pm	pm	pm	am			K			am			K	am	am						SX	SO	SO	SX	N	C	am
LONDON (King's X) dep		7c25	7c40		8c25	10c35	10c45	1 5			K			am			4 45	4 45			10 5						1050	1120	11 30			7j25
York	103	11c16	11c31		11f50	1a11	2a55	3a17	4 55								9 30	9 38			11 7							1144	12p11	12p21	
Darlington		10d44			2 13	3 8	4 14	5 48						8 35			9 57	9 57			11 7										

		am	am	MX am	am	am	am	am	am	am	X am	am	am	am		am	am	am	am	am	am	pm	pm		pm	pm	pm	pm	pm	pm	pm
NEWCASTLE Central dep		1 0	1 15	1 34	3 15	4 45	6 13	7 0			7 40	8 15		9 32		10 8	11 21	1110	1123	1212		1223	1238	1242	1 5	1 15					
Manors East "																						1225	1240								
Heaton "						6 18					8 21				1010		1129				1229	1244								
Forest Hall "						6 25				8 28				1014		1136				1236	1251								
Killingworth "						6 28				8 31				1021		1139				1239	1254								
Annitsford "						6 33				8 36				1024		1144				1244	1259								
Cramlington "						6 39				8 42				1029						1259	1 5								
Plessey "										8 46				1035						1 3	1 9								
Stannington "						6 46				8 51				1039		1150				1 8	1 14								
Morpeth arr			3 41			6 51				8 58	9 57	9 57		1044				12 2	1237		1 13	1 19								
Morpeth dep			3 43			6 54				8 7	9 4	9 59		1049			12 4	1239											
Pegswood "						7 0				9 9			1050																
Longhirst "						7 6				9 13			1054																
Widdrington "						7 12				9 21			1058				1214												
Chevington "						7 18				9 28			11 4																
Acklington "						7 21				9 37			1110				1224												
Warkworth "										9 44			1116				1230												
Alnmouth arr			4 7			7 29	7 44	7 35		8 30	9 50	1022		1122				1235	2										
Alnmouth dep			4 9				7 45	7 50		8 32	9 58	1024		1130				1237	5	1 15	1 37								
Longhoughton "											10 4								2 11	1 43								
Little Mill "											10 9								2 17	1 26	2 11							
Christon Bank "								8 3			1015		1040						3 21	7 17								
Chathill "								8 9			1024								3 82	2 23								
Newham "											1028								4 12	2 26								
Lucker "								8 15			1033								4 62	2 31								
Belford "								8 23		8 56	1038		1050		11 0				5 12	2 36								
Beal "								8 33					11 0		11 1				2 46									
Goswick "								8 38							1116				2 6	2 51								
Scremerston "								8 44							1122				2 12	2 57								
Tweedmouth "								8 49	8 59						1131				2 19	3 4								
Berwick B arr			4 48	6 10		8 21		9 2	9 15		1113	1134				1 51	2 23	3 7		2	2 25	2 35							
Berwick dep			4 54	6 12		8 23		9 18			1117								2	5 27	2 37								
Dunbar arr			8k10		8 59			9 54			1155						2 41	3 2	3 13									
Drem A arr			7g 1		10n57			10e25			1211							4e 9										
EDINBURGH (Waverley)		3 35	3 50	4 0	6 6	7 30	9 36		10 33		1238			1 27	1 35		3 21	3 40	3 50									

A For complete service between Berwick and Edinburgh see Scottish Area Time Table.
B For other trains between Tweedmouth and Berwick see Table 168.
C Saturdays only. Runs 22nd July to 19th August inclusive.
K Saturdays only and not after 2nd September.
MX Mondays excepted.
N Saturdays only and not after 9th September.

SO Saturdays only.
SX Saturdays excepted.
X One class only.
a am.
c Also applies on Sunday nights.
d On Sunday nights leaves 10-33 pm.
e Change at Dunbar.
f Sunday nights excepted.

g On Saturdays until 16th September inclusive calls at Drem to set down passengers from King's Cross. On other days calls when required to set down passengers from King's Cross.
h Arrives Little Mill 1-48 pm.
j On Saturdays leaves King's Cross 7-30 pm.
k Change at Berwick.
n Change at Dunbar. On Saturdays arrives 10-25 am.
p pm.

Figure 9.2. (continued on next page) The summer 1939 timetable for Down trains, which, if Germany had not invaded Poland, would have been in operation until 24 instead of curtailed to 3 September. Unlike later BR services there are only five named trains over the line: the 'Highlandman' and 'Aberdonian' sleeping car trains served Glasgow and Aberdeen respectively; the 'Queen of Scots' Pullman and 'Coronation' had supplementary charges, but the non-stop 'Flying Scotsman' only required ordinary fares. Virtually every long-distance train had restaurant or buffet car services.

between Alnwick or Morpeth and Newcastle. The 2010 timetable gives the normal daily service between Newcastle and Edinburgh as 34 trains each way and, though very good for through passengers, it is not so good for local trips. There are 13 options from Morpeth to Alnmouth with the best taking 15 minutes. However, seven of these require backtracking to Newcastle, take over an hour and cost nearly twice as much!

The decline in passenger travel across BR during the 1960s and 70s provoked a report by civil servant Sir David Serpell in 1983, which said that the Newcastle to Edinburgh, as well as other main routes, should be closed completely. Fortunately this did not happen and the long-awaited electrification went ahead to give the results we see today.

Table 157—continued. NEWCASTLE, MORPETH, ALNMOUTH, BERWICK, DUNBAR AND EDINBURGH.

WEEKDAYS—continued

(Timetable detail — principal stations Newcastle (Central / Manors East), Heaton, Forest Hall, Killingworth, Annitsford, Cramlington, Plessey, Stannington, Morpeth (arr/dep), Pegswood, Longhirst, Widdrington, Chevington, Acklington, Warkworth, Alnmouth (arr/dep), Longhoughton, Little Mill, Christon Bank, Chathill, Newham, Lucker, Belford, Beal, Goswick, Scremerston, Tweedmouth, Berwick (arr/dep), Dunbar (arr), Drem, Edinburgh (Waverley). Columns note trains such as "THE FLYING SCOTSMAN", "THE QUEEN OF SCOTS", "THE CORONATION", and Restaurant Car / Pullman Car services.)

A For complete service between Berwick and Edinburgh see Scottish Area Time Table.
B For other trains between Tweedmouth and Berwick see Table 168.
C Saturdays only. Runs 15th July to 26th August inclusive.
D Saturdays excepted. Does not run Friday 4th and Monday 7th August.
E Runs Mondays 24th July to 28th August, Fridays 14th July to 25th August and Saturdays until 16th September inclusive.
F Saturdays excepted. Commencing 11th September runs every weekday.

G Calls at Dunbar 9-45 pm when required to set down passengers from Newcastle and South thereof.
J Does not run on Saturdays 15th July to 26th August inclusive.
K Saturdays only and not after 2nd September.
N Saturdays only and not after 9th September.
SO Saturdays only.
SX Saturdays excepted.
W Calls to set down only.
X One class only.
b Saturdays excepted and not after 8th September, also runs Saturday, 16th September.
c Change at Dunbar.

d On Saturdays leaves York 1-45 and Darlington 2-37 pm. (From 15th July to 26th August leaves York 1-53 and Darlington 2-46 pm).
g On Saturdays leaves York 4-56 and Darlington 5-48 pm.
h On 8th July and 9th September leaves Darlington 6-2 pm.
p pm.
u pm. By ordinary train York to Darlington.
v Calls at Drem only when required to set down passengers.
y Commences 11th September.

Table 157—continued. NEWCASTLE, MORPETH, ALNMOUTH, BERWICK, DUNBAR AND EDINBURGH.

WEEKDAYS—continued | *SUNDAYS*

(Timetable detail — same station list; Sunday columns include "SUNDAY SCOTSMAN" and Restaurant Car services, plus trains routed to Edinburgh via Galashiels through the Buffet Car service.)

A For complete service between Berwick and Edinburgh see Scottish Area Time Table.
B For other trains between Tweedmouth and Berwick see Table 168.
C Commences 17th September.
E Calls at Dunbar 9-56 pm on 9th July and commencing 3rd September.
SO Saturdays only.
SX Saturdays excepted.

T Not after 27th August.
V Runs 16th July to 27th August inclusive.
Y Not after 10th September.
b am.
b On 16th and 23rd September leaves York 6-12 and Darlington 7-1 pm.
c Calls at Drem when required to set down passengers from King's Cross.
d Arrives Chevington 7-8 pm.

f Friday 4th and Monday 7th August excepted, passengers can leave King's Cross 4-0 pm and York 6-40 pm by "The Coronation." Supplementary charges. Limited accommodation. (See Cream Inset).
j Does not run Friday 4th and Monday 7th August. "The Silver Jubilee." Supplementary charges. Limited accommodation. (See Cream Inset).
t Saturday nights.

Goods Traffic

TE Harrison's forecast of 1,000 tons of goods passing over the line daily seems to be reasonable for the early years. Even prior to the First World War, around a dozen through and local freight trains a day, in each direction, were all that was shown in the working timetables, but there were numerous coal trains serving the collieries to the south of Alnmouth. In 1913, Tweedmouth shed handled 20 freight diagrams per day; this included the Kelso Branch goods and the additional fish and cattle trains running as necessary on the main line. Fish traffic really built up during the First World War; it was generally southbound with some conveyed by special trains and smaller quantities attached to passenger trains. During the 1880s the 5-10 pm from Edinburgh was described as a 'fast passenger and fish' even though it stopped at every station between Edinburgh and Berwick plus another five before Newcastle, and took 4 hours 45 minutes over the 124-mile journey (26 mph); it remained the only through passenger train to be worked by an NBR engine as far as Berwick until the dispute of 1897.

Through 'Aberdeen Express Goods' were soon to appear in the working timetables, and in the summer of 1856 a weekly 'Aberdeen Express Cattle' was added for a few months. (Figure 9.3) The word 'express' was a misnomer with journey times of around 43 hours (13 mph) between Aberdeen and London (Camden), and 7 hours less to King's Cross, but they were a lot faster than the alternative of using steamships. Meat, and later fish, travelling south and perishables going north gave a considerable boost to the economy of north-east Scotland. By the 1860s two 'Aberdeen Express Goods' had been established, leaving Berwick southbound at 5-45 and 6-30 am and Newcastle northbound at 2-45 and 11-0 pm each day. By the 1880s their schedules to King's Cross had been reduced by around 8 hours and the reinstatement of the Tay Bridge and the opening of the Forth Bridge in 1890 allowed further savings in time and distance.

Considerably improved timings, most beneficial to long-distance trains carrying perishable goods, could have resulted from the wagons being fitted with continuous brakes, but with the Great Northern using vacuum and the NER and NBR using Westinghouse air brakes few wagons were dual fitted; thus the introduction of fitted trains was slow. Locomotives working the East-Coast express passenger services had been dual fitted since the late 1870s, and when relegated to more mundane duties were able to haul GNR braked-goods trains off its territory. The 1908 working timetable shows the advantages with the GNR 'Braked Scotch Goods' taking under 4 hours from York to Berwick whilst the unfitted 'Aberdeen Goods' took nearly 8 hours for the 147 miles. After grouping the LNER became a vacuum-braked line, and a large number of wagons were equipped, allowing much faster services with 'fully fitted' or 'part fitted' goods trains; the fish trains from Aberdeen were then taking under $13\frac{1}{2}$ hours to reach the capital.

With the line serving a rural area, not a lot of local traffic was handled; domestic coal, animal feeds, fertiliser, farm machinery, young livestock, groceries and manufactured goods were received at the intermediate stations, and mature livestock, agricultural produce and quarried stone were the main items forwarded. The Beeching Report of 1963 put the freight tonnage carried over the line in excess of 100,000 tons per week, and the contribution from most local stations less than 5,000 tons *per annum;* only Morpeth, Amble, Alnwick and Tweedmouth handled more than 25,000 tons. Following the implementation of the Report, freight traffic almost disappeared from the railway. The little that remains of the Anglo-Scottish freight goes via the West Coast Main Line with only the odd coal, alumina, cement or tank train travelling between Berwick and Morpeth or Tyne Yard.[6]

Plate 9.2. Belford, looking south on 30 October 1959. The goods facilities provided upon the opening of the line more or less sufficed at most wayside stations until closure. Belford would close to goods traffic on 7 June 1965. For a diagram of the sidings at Belford, see Appendix 5. (John F Mallon / Joint NERA - Ken Hoole Study Centre John Mallon Collection)

Goods, Cattle, & Mineral Trains between Berwick & Newcastle. 3

MILES.	UP.	1 Thro' Goods.	2 Aberdeen Exp. Cattle.	3 Aberd'n Express Goods.	4 Pick-up & Thro' Goods.	5 Coal. Pick-up.	6 Coke.	7 Thro' Goods.	8 Thro' Meat Train.	SUNDAYS. 1 Meat Train.	SUNDAYS. 2 Aberd'n Express Goods.
		A.M.	A.M.	A.M.	A.M.	P.M.	P.M.	P.M.	P.M.	P.M.	A.M.
	BERWICK	2 0	5 45	8 15	...	...	2 0	3 0	10 15	10 15	8 15
1¼	Tweedmouth	2 15	...	...	8 30	1 30	...	3 20	11 30	11 30	...
3½	Scremerston	...	...	...	8 40	1 42	...	...	...	...	...
8½	Beal	...	...	...	9 0	2 7	...	...	...	...	...
15½	Belford	3 0	...	...	9 30	2 42	...	4 0	...	This Train does not run on Sunday nights.	...
17¾	Lucker	...	...	...	9 40	2 54	...	...	...		...
19¾	Newham	...	...	...	9 50	3 4	...	...	...		...
21	Chathill	...	...	...	10 5	3 11	...	...	...		...
24	Christon Bank	...	...	...	10 25	3 26	...	...	...		...
29¼	Longhoughton	...	...	...	10 45	3 52	...	...	...		...
32	Bilton	4 0	7 30	10 0	11 5	4 5	4 0	5 0	...		10 0
	Alnwick Arr.	This Train does not run regularly on Mondays.	...	This Train does not run on Mondays.	12 20	...	...	...	...		...
35	Alnwick Dep.		Runs on Fridays only.		...	...	...	...	...		...
35	Warkworth				11 20	4 20	...	...	...		...
38½	Acklington				11 35	4 37	...	...	...		...
43¾	Widdrington				11 50	5 4	...	...	...		...
46¾	Longhirst				12 10	5 19	...	...	...		...
50¼	Morpeth	5 30			12 50	6 23	...	6 30	...		...
53	Netherton	...			1 5	6 34	...	...	...		...
57	Cramlington	...			1 20	6 54	...	...	...		...
61	Killingworth	...			1 40	7 15	...	...	...		...
	Benton	...			...	...	...	...	...		...
65¼	Heaton	...	...		...	7 35	...	...	...	...	...
67	NEWCASTLE ... Arr	6 30	9 30	11 45	2 15	7 45	6 15	7 30	3 30	3 30	11 45

Goods, Cattle, & Mineral Trains between Newcastle & Berwick.

MILES.	DOWN.	1 Coal.	2 Pick-up Goods.	3 Thro' Goods.	4 Coke.	5 Aberdeen Exp. Goods.	6 Thro' Goods.	7 Thro' Goods.	8	SUNDAYS. 1 Thro' GOODS.	SUNDAYS. 2
		A.M.	A.M.	A.M.	P.M.	P.M.	P.M.	P.M		P.M.	
	NEWCASTLE...Dep.	5 0	6 50	8 30	1 40	2 30	3 45	8 0	...	7 0	...
	Heaton	5 10	...	...	...	...	...	...	...	...	...
	Benton	...	...	...	...	...	...	...	...	...	...
	Killingworth	6 20	7 10	...	...	...	...	...	...	...	...
	Cramlington	6 40	7 25	...	...	...	...	...	...	...	...
	Netherton	7 50	7 35	...	...	...	...	...	...	...	...
	Morpeth	7 10	8 15	9 30	...	...	4 45	9 0	...	...	...
	Longhirst	7 25	8 30	...	...	...	...	...	...	...	...
	Widdrington	7 40	8 45	...	...	...	...	...	...	...	...
	Acklington	8 0	9 0	...	...	...	...	...	...	...	...
	Warkworth	9 15	9 15	...	...	...	...	...	...	...	...
	Bilton	9 5	9 40	10 30	4 0	4 25	6 5	9 55	...	...	...
	Alnwick Arr.	...	...	...	...	...	...	10 15	...	...	...
	Alnwick Dep.	...	...	...	...	...	...	...	...	...	...
	Longhoughton	9 20	9 55	...	...	...	...	...	...	...	...
	Christon Bank	9 45	10 25	...	...	...	...	...	...	...	...
	Chathill	10 0	10 45	...	...	...	...	...	...	...	...
	Newham	10 10	10 55	...	...	...	...	...	...	...	...
	Lucker	10 22	11 10	...	...	...	...	...	...	...	...
	Belford	10 50	11 35	11 30	...	...	...	11 5	...	...	...
	Beal	11 15	12 0	...	...	...	...	...	...	...	...
	Scremerston	11 30	12 15	...	...	...	...	...	...	...	...
	Tweedmouth	11 45	12 30	12 50	...	...	7 50	12 0	...	...	...
	BERWICK	...	12 45	1 0	6 0	6 15	8 0	...	...	11 0	...

Figure 9.3. *The working timetable for freight trains for May 1856. (Courtesy of David and Claire Williamson)*

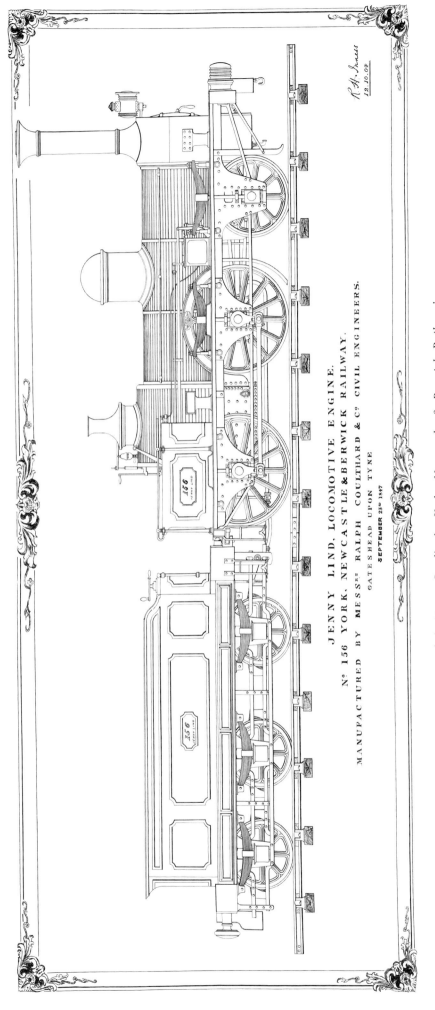

JENNY LIND, LOCOMOTIVE ENGINE.

Nº 156 YORK, NEWCASTLE & BERWICK RAILWAY.

MANUFACTURED BY MESSʳˢ RALPH COULTHARD & Cᵒ CIVIL ENGINEERS.

GATESHEAD UPON TYNE

SEPTEMBER 23ᴿᴰ 1847

Figure 9.4. *'Jenny Lind', the York, Newcastle & Berwick Railway's No 156, and one of two locomotives built to this design by Coulthard's. (The second, No 5, was built in June 1849.) No 156 retained this number when it was taken into the stock of the newly-formed North Eastern Railway; as, indeed did all of the YN&B's locomotives. Driving wheels were 5' 0" diameter; note that the leading driving wheels are flangeless. No 156 was replaced in 1875. (RH Inness / NERA Collection)*

Locomotives

It is almost sufficient to say that the locomotives got bigger, and generally better, to match increasing train loads and demands for higher speeds. The history of North Eastern locomotives has been adequately covered in books ranging from JS MacLean's *Locomotives of the North Eastern Railway* of 1925 to *North Eastern Record Volume 3* published in 2000; the later ones are adequately expounded in *Locomotives of the LNER* and books and articles by CJ Allen, OS Nock and WB Yeadon.

Most NER, LNER and BR classes put in an appearance on the line. A Riddles class 9F 2-10-0 even worked passenger trains on the Alnwick Branch for the last day of steam on 18 June 1966, and, at the other extreme, one of the diminutive class Y7 0-4-0 dock tanks was allocated to Tweedmouth in November 1948 to work the North Sunderland Railway until its closure on 28 October 1951.

The York, Newcastle & Berwick Railway had around 200 locomotives in 1849; most of the passenger ones were 'singles' of the 2-2-2 wheel arrangement, and the goods 0-6-0s. Soon the 2-4-0 was to become the standard for passenger trains (Figure 9.4 and Plates 9.4 and 9.5), and it was not until 1884 that 4-4-0s started to run on the line. The first 4-6-0s were introduced in 1899, the Atlantics followed four years later, and Pacifics of NER and GNR designs appeared in 1922. Neither Pacific was very successful when built, but the Gresley version was much easier to improve into an outstanding machine, which put in almost 40 years service on express passenger working; most of the earlier classes survived for little more than a decade before being superseded by the 'latest model' on top-link duties. Articles and books by Allen, Nock and others have included logs of runs on normal passenger services or on test trains over the Newcastle and Berwick for those that are interested.

The majority of freight, into the early twentieth century, was handled by 0-6-0 locomotives, and the type continued to handle coal and mineral traffic until the end of steam in 1967. Some 0-6-0s with driving wheel diameters in excess of five feet were fitted with Westinghouse brakes for working local passenger trains and braked-goods, and a few were dual fitted to handle the GNR goods. Former passenger locomotives were relegated to freight duties, and numerous mixed-traffic types of 4-6-0, 2-6-0 and 2-6-2 wheel arrangements handled most of the later through traffic on the line. The advent of diesels coincided with the rapid decline of freight on the railways, and now the Newcastle and Berwick passenger traffic has a virtual monopoly, which greatly simplifies the operation of the line.

Endnotes:
1. Hoole, K. *The Illustrated History of East Coast Joint Stock* (1993) page 10, 21.
2. Tomlinson, WW. *The North Eastern Railway: its Rise and Development* (1914) pages 735-741, also Nock, OS, *Railway Race to the North* (1958).
3. Hoole, K. *North Eastern Locomotive Sheds* (1972) page 54.
4. Tomlinson *op. cit.* page 741-2.
5. Allen, CJ. *The London & North Eastern Railway* (1966) page 199-200. From July 1937 the 'Coronation' was allowed to further reduce the time to 6 hours.
6. Rawlinson, M. *2010 National Freight Timetable No 58.*

Various public and working timetables published between 1847 and 2010 have been referred to.

Plate 9.3. This locomotive was re-built by R Stephenson & Company in December 1853 from a 2-4-0 of 1847 to the 2-2-2 seen here. The York, Newcastle & Berwick Railway numbered it 159, which number it kept on the North Eastern Railway until February 1885 when it was transferred from the capital stock list to the duplicate list and re-numbered 1709. As seen here, the locomotive has undergone changes since re-building: a cab has replaced the original weatherboard; a new boiler and chimney, a larger sandbox and an air compressor have been fitted; the driving wheel splasher, originally pierced, has been sheeted in. Note the careful finish applied to the tallow polish to the paintwork – a finish marred by the loss of paint from the boiler. (NERA Valentine Rippon Collection)

Plate 9.4. *No 25, the first of its class introduced in 1862, was the first NER locomotive to run through from Newcastle to Edinburgh following the 1869 agreement. Pictured at York is its sister engine No 26. (NERA Ken Hoole Collection)*

Plate 9.5. *The more powerful 901 class 2-4-0, of 1872, was the last express passenger class to be introduced by Edward Fletcher. It was intended to haul heavier and faster main-line expresses, but by the mid 1880s even longer trains meant that the locomotives often had to work in pairs. They were gradually superseded by 4-4-0s, and spent their remaining lives on branch-line services. The first of the class is seen at Edinburgh in its heyday. (NERA Ken Hoole Collection)*

Plate 9.6. *Class Q (D17/2) No 1906 seen on an Up stopping train at Forest Hall in the 1930s. (EE Smith)*

Plate 9.7. *The class R (D20) of 1899 outlived all the later NER express locomotives. They did yeoman service on the Newcastle & Berwick, on all types of trains, and the last six of the class were not withdrawn from Alnmouth shed until 1957. No 2105, well past its heyday, is seen with a stopping passenger train at Craigentinny (on the North British Section) in the late 1920s / early 1930s. (J Robertson / NERA Tom Smeaton Collection)*

Plate 9.8. *The class S (B13), introduced in 1899, was the first British 4-6-0 designed for passenger work. They were intended for use on the heavier trains between Newcastle and Edinburgh to avoid double-heading, but, unlike their contemporary class R, they were not a success. By the time the class of 40 locomotives was completed in 1909 they were almost exclusively employed on perishable and excursion traffic. At Grouping Tweedmouth and Heaton sheds each had eight of the class. No 752 is seen at an unidentified location on freight train; the locomotive would be withdrawn in June 1934. (NERA Tom Smeaton Collection)*

Plate 9.9. *Class V (C6) No 784 on an express goods at Tweedmouth in early LNER days. (J Robertson / NERA Tom Smeaton Collection)*

Plate 9.10. *Class Z (C7) No 2211 seen at Longhirst on 21 April 1919 southbound with a train of empty coaching stock. (NERA Tom Smeaton Collection)*

Plate 9.11. *A classic postcard view of Gresley A1 Pacific 'Night Hawk' accelerating the Up 'Flying Scotsman' across the Royal Border Bridge, probably in the summer of 1925. The locomotive had been completed by the North British Locomotive Company in the previous October, and was allocated to Gateshead shed. The lettering on the buffer beam describes it as 'Class 4.6.2'. (Author's Collection)*

Plate 9.12. *35 years later, 'Night Hawk', now class A3 No 60078, has been sidetracked on to the Up loop at Belford before making its scheduled 12-33 pm stop there on 30 March 1960. (Dr GES McDonald)*

Plate 9.13. *A class V2 hauls a Down express through Chathill circa 1950, while class Y7 No 68089, on hire to the North Sunderland Railway, waits to take the next train to Seahouses. (WA Camwell)*

Plate 9.14. *Class V2 No 60952 passes Acklington at the head of a Down express goods on 1 September 1959. (Neville Stead)*

Plate 9.15. A busy summer's day on the Newcastle & Berwick; class A4 No 60012 'Commonwealth of Australia' passes through Longhoughton on 6 July 1953 with the second Up 'Flying Scotsman'. (John F Mallon / Joint NERA - Ken Hoole Study Centre Collection)

Plate 9.16. Class B1 61025 'Pallah' is seen at Alnmouth on the 6-05 pm ex Newcastle on 2 May 1953. At that time it was allocated to Tweedmouth shed, which had three daily, main-line passenger turns rostered for the class, two to Newcastle and one to Edinburgh. (John F Mallon / Joint NERA - Ken Hoole Study Centre Collection)

Plate 9.17. Peppercorn class A1 No 60142 'Edward Fletcher' passing Little Mill on the Up 'Flying Scotsman' on 26 June 1953. (John F Mallon / Joint NERA - Ken Hoole Study Centre Collection)

Plate 9.18. *No 183 was one of two goods locomotives supplied to the York, Newcastle & Berwick Railway in July 1848 by Nasmyth Gaskell & Company. It is seen here in service with the North Eastern Railway, fitted with a cab and Fletcher-style dome and chimney. The locomotive does, however, retain its YN&B pattern numberplate. No 183 was replaced in 1881. (NERA Valentine Rippon Collection)*

Plate 9.19. *No 231 was one of batch of fifteen goods locomotives ordered by the York, Newcastle & Berwick Railway from EB Wilson & Company; it was delivered in June 1854 and is seen here in service with the North Eastern Railway, fitted with Fletcher-style chimney and a cab replacing the original weatherboard. No 231 was re-numbered to 1704 in the duplicate list in 1885, soldiering on for a few more years before final withdrawal in 1888. Note the lack of any 'North Eastern Railway' lettering or even initials on either locomotive or tender in the company's early years. (NERA Valentine Rippon Collection)*

Plate 9.20. *The 0-6-0 type was, and would be even after the introduction of the 0-8-0 in 1901, the mainstay of the North Eastern's goods and mineral traffic. No 627 was built at the company's Gateshead Works in February 1876. It is seen here post re-building with a Worsdell boiler in August 1891. The locomotive worked until withdrawal in December 1924. 0-6-0s fitted with Westinghouse air brakes were also used by the North Eastern for excursion traffic, and sister locomotive to No 627 – No 1451 – was involved in an accident when hauling such a train on 26 October 1898. No 1451 was departing Newcastle Central with a Sunderland - Alnwick excursion comprising 16 Third Class carriages full of excursionists when it collided with a light engine. Five passengers and a guard suffered minor injuries and two of the carriages were de-railed. Whether the excursionists ever got to Alnwick is not known. (NERA Ken Hoole Collection)*

Plate 9.21. *No 1549 was built March 1891 at the NER's Darlington Works as a two-cylinder compound of class C. It is still running as a compound here, but would be re-built as a two-cylinder simple in March 1904. Note the air compressor, installed to power the air brakes of summer excursion trains. The LNER re-classified the locomotive J21, and ran it until until withdrawal in February 1937. (NERA Ken Hoole Collection)*

Plate 9.22. *The first of the NER's class P3 to be built was No 790, which rolled out of Darlington Works in April 1906. It is seen here as BR's class J27 No 65780, working an Up coal train through Heaton on 17 August 1959. (NE Stead Collection)*

Plate 9.23. *Tweedmouth class K3 No 61984 heads an Up goods through Killingworth. (JW Armstrong / Armstrong Railway Photographic Trust)*

Plate 9.24. Class K1 No 62024 shunting at Belford on 14 July 1966. The 30,000 gallon water tank on the right was supplied by Richardson & Son of Castle Eden in 1848. (John M Fleming)

Plate 9.25. During LNER days Tweedmouth had a least three class J77 tank engines allocated for shunting duties. No 68421 is seen on 22 August 1953 less than a year before it was withdrawn. All the class were rebuilds of 0-4-4 Bogie Tank Passenger (BTP) engines. (John F Mallon)

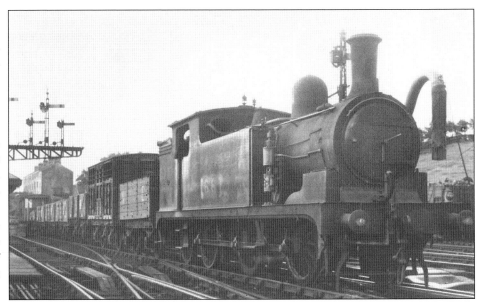

Plate 9.26. (Right) Class N10 No 1667 seen on a short goods train at Alnmouth on 11 August 1939. (NERA Tom Smeaton Collection)

Plate 9.27. (Below) Tweedmouth did not get a class G5 allocated until 1947. Here we see No 67269, still with a Blaydon shed plate, working the Kelso Branch train on 12 June 1954. (J Robertson / NERA Tom Smeaton Collection)

Plate 9.28. (Below) The pick-up freight heading for Tweedmouth passes Norham on 26 September 1964 with BR Standard 2MT No 78024 running tender-first. The 1902 signal cabin replaced the one seen in Plate 7.3 and still exists today as part of a small museum at Norham station; it has the gabled roof which came into use around this time. The goods yard is partly visible on the left. Despite the Up Home signal No 19 (in the background) being at 'clear', the train is really a 'stop and examine' candidate as no-one has placed an appropriate headlamp on the right above the tender buffer beam – perhaps the lamp is still on the front of the locomotive. (JC Dean)

ACKLINGTON STATION

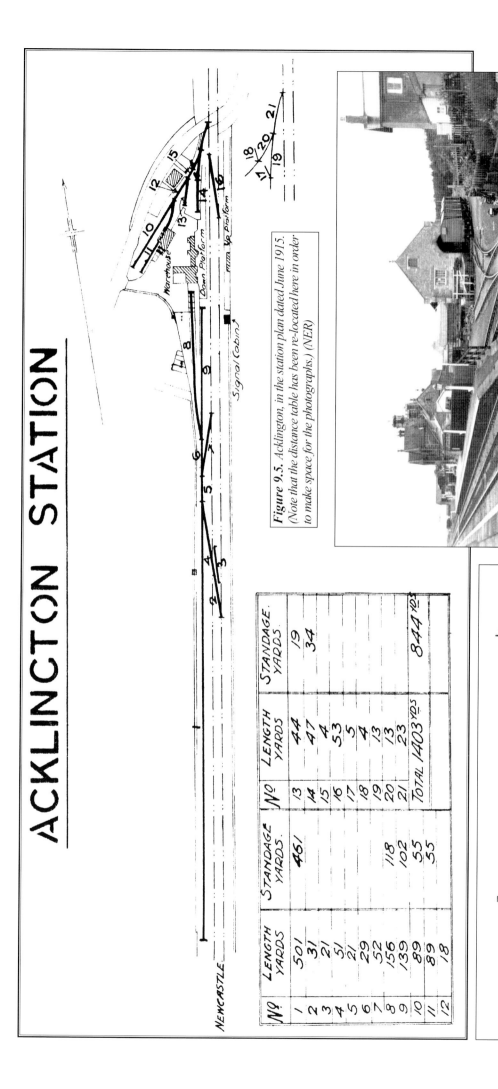

Nº	LENGTH YARDS	STANDAGE YARDS.
1	501	461
2	31	
3	21	
4	51	
5	21	
6	29	
7	52	
8	156	118
9	139	102
10	89	55
11	89	55
12	18	

Nº	LENGTH YARDS	STANDAGE YARDS.
13	44	19
14	47	34
15	4	
16	53	
17	5	
18	4	
19	13	
20	13	
21	23	
TOTAL	1403 YDS	844 YDS

Figure 9.5. Acklington, in the station plan dated June 1915. (Note that the distance table has been re-located here in order to make space for the photographs.) (NER)

Plates 9.29 and 9.30. Acklington, viewed from the south (left) and the north (above) on 27 October 1959. For further views of the station, see Figure 5.4 and Plates 5.4, 5.14, 5.18 and 9.14. (John F Mallon / Joint NERA - Ken Hoole Study Centre Collection)

Appendix 1

Newcastle & Berwick Railway.

Miles and chains of stations on the line with opening and closing dates for passengers and closing dates for goods.
(There are 80 chains of 66 feet to a mile.) From information provided by Alan Young.

M Chs	Station	Opened	Closed passengers	Closed goods
0-00	**NEWCASTLE CENTRAL**	30 August 1850	Open	
0-45	**CARLIOL SQUARE N&NS**	20 June 1839	30 August 1850	
0-45.91	**MANORS EAST**	30 August 1850	Open	
1-43	**HEATON** (First)	By January 1856	1 March 1887	
1-51.46	**HEATON** (Second)	1 March 1887	11 August 1980	
5-1.02	**FOREST HALL**	February 1856	15 September 1958	15 September 1958
5-71.40	**KILLINGWORTH**	1 March 1847	15 September 1958	7 June 1965
7-56.90	**ANNITSFORD**	8 July 1878	15 September 1958	11 November 1963
7-70	**DUDLEY COLLIERY**	April 1860	8 July 1878	
9-74.05	**CRAMLINGTON**	1 March 1847	Open	4 July 1966
11-41.18	**PLESSEY**	July 1859	15 September 1958	2 April 1962
13-71.81	**STANNINGTON**	1 March 1847	15 September 1958	10 August 1964
16-49.60	**MORPETH**	1 March 1847	Open	
18-43.86	**PEGSWOOD**	1 January 1903	Open	10 August 1964
19-11	**ASHINGTON COL. JCN.**	December 1871	August 1878	
20-14.04	**LONGHIRST**	1 July 1847	29 October 1951	10 August 1964
23-20.31	**WIDDRINGTON**	1 July 1847	Open	28 December 1964
25-48.43	**CHEVINGTON**	October 1870	15 September 1958	10 August 1964
28-42.67	**ACKLINGTON**	1 July 1847	Open	5 September 1966
31-76.07	**WARKWORTH**	1 July 1847	15 September 1958	2 April 1962
34-69.12	**ALNMOUTH**	1 October 1850?	Open	
36-52	**LESBURY**	1 July 1847	October 1850?	
37-38.88	**LONGHOUGHTON**	1 July 1847	18 June 1962	18 June 1962
39-36.51	**LITTLE MILL**	January 1861	15 September 1958	7 June 1965
43-2.79	**CHRISTON BANK**	1 July 1847	15 September 1958	7 June 1965
43-49.54	**FALLODON** *Private Station*	1 July 1847	30 May 1934	
46-2.91	**CHATHILL**	29 March 1847	Open	7 June 1965
47-9.87	**NEWHAM**	February 1851	25 September 1950	25 September 1950
49-19.91	**LUCKER**	29 March 1847	2 February 1953	7 June 1965
51-51.53	**BELFORD**	29 March 1847	29 January 1968	7 June 1965
52-47	**CRAG MILL**	February 1871	October 1877	
55-1.80	**SMEAFIELD**	February 1871	1 May 1930	
58-49.36	**BEAL**	29 March 1947	29 January 1968	26 April 1965
60-67.17	**GOSWICK**	November 1870	15 September 1958	10 August 1964
63-48.72	**SCREMERSTON**	29 March 1847	8 July 1951	8 July 1951
65-64.89	**TWEEDMOUTH**	29 March 1847	15 June 1964	
67-0.02	**BERWICK-UPON-TWEED**	22 June 1846	Open	

Appendix 1 Remarks:

Figures in italics are the approximate mileages of stations closed prior to 1900.

Name changes:

Heaton was also known as 'Heaton for Byker'.

Forest Hall was renamed from Benton on 1 December 1874.

Stannington was renamed from Netherton on 1 January 1892.

Alnmouth was known as Bilton Junction then Bilton until renamed Alnmouth on 2 May 1892.

Goswick was renamed from Windmill Hill on 1 January 1898.

Closures during the Second World War:

Longhoughton, Little Mill, Newham, Lucker, Goswick and Scemerston closed to passengers from 5 May 1941 until 7 October 1946.

Appendix 2

Kelso Branch.

Miles and chains of features on the line.

Note: DP = Distance Point; a cast-iron sign marked the centre point of the station.

M Chs	Feature
0-00	**Tweedmouth North Junction**
2-36.46	**West Ord Siding Dwarf Frame**
4-4.16	**VELVET HALL DP** Closed 4 July 1955
4-6.47	**Velvet Hall Signal Cabin**
6-59.23	**NORHAM DP** Closed 15 June 1964
6-62.41	**Norham Signal Cabin**
7-41.31	**Newbiggin Dene Viaduct**
9-46.71	**Twizell Signal Cabin**
9-50.16	**TWIZELL DP** Closed 4 July 1855
10-10.25	**River Till Viaduct**
12-18.24	**Dwarf Lever Frame**
12-39.66	**Coldstream Signal Cabin**
12-40.53	**COLDSTREAM DP** Closed 15 June 1964
12-44.33	**Junction with the Alnwick & Cornhill**
13-56.00	**East Learmouth Viaduct**
13-78.31	**West Learmouth Viaduct**
14-20.68	**Learmouth Siding Signal Cabin**
15-45.44	**Sunilaws Signal Cabin**
15-46.32	**SUNILAWS DP** Closed 4 July 1955
17-17.78	**BR Regional Boundary Down Line**
17-17.86	**Private Siding Dwarf Frame**
17-19.00	**BR Regional Boundary Up Line**
17-51.97	**ENGLAND/SCOTLAND Border**
17-68.30	**CARHAM DP** Closed 4 July 1955
17-68.74	**Carham Signal Cabin**
20-5.32	**Sprouston Signal Cabin**
20-12.77	**SPROUSTON DP** Closed 4 July 1955
21-12.86	**Former NER/NBR Boundary Down Line**
21-12.96	**Former NER/NBR Boundary Up line**
22-30.99	**NBR Kelso Signal Cabin**
22-34.26	**NBR KELSO Station** Closed 15 June 1964

Appendix 3A

Signalling Installations, Newcastle - Berwick

Mileage (M Chns)	Name	Opened	Closed	Cabin Type and Location	Lever Frame / Panel	Remarks
-	Tyneside IECC	19-22.4.1991		Gateshead	IECC	Newcastle Work Station (controls as far as Plessey crossovers).
0.00	Newcastle PSB	12.4.1959	19.4.1991	Above Platform 10 and carriage sidings	OCS Panel	Mileage estimated. Replaced Newcastle Nos 1, 2, 3 and Manors station SBs. AWS between Newcastle and Alnmouth 5/6.1.1963. Replaced by Tyneside IECC.
0.02	Newcastle No 1 SB (1)	1871	1894?	Platform 8	18	May have become No 2 SB (2) in 1894.
0.02	Newcastle No 2 SB (2)	1894 or earlier see above	12.04.1959	Non-standard timber Platform 8	Mech frame: unknown. EP: 67, Style B	May have been the former No.1 (1) structure. Converted to EP frame, 1907. Replaced by Newcastle PSB. Structure destroyed by fire, 1961.
0.05	Newcastle No 2 SB (1)	1871	1893	Early N5 overhead	37	Mileage estimated. Bridge cabin at east end of Platform No 8.
0.13	Newcastle No 1 SB (3)	12.11.1909	12.04.1959	N5 Overhead (Up)	283 Style B EP	259 working levers, reduced to 198 working by 1958. Semaphores replaced by colour light signals July 1953. Replaced by Newcastle PSB.
0.15	Newcastle No 1 SB (2)	1893	12.11.1909	N1 special, stone (Down)	244	Mileage estimated.
0.15	Newcastle No 3 SB (1)	1871	1893	Early N5 overhead	57 in 1871, 77 in 1882	Mileage estimated. Also known as 'Cast e Jct'.
c 0.18	Octagon / Castle Jct	by 12.6.1887	1891	Special (Up)		In 1858 this junction was controlled from 'Castle Jnc Huts 1, 2 and 3'. Octagonal building is shown on 1862 1:500 OS Map.
0.25	Dean Street SB	1889 - 1895	Nov-09	N6 Cantilever built on parapet (Up)	30 McK&H, Stevens locking	Also 'Dene Street'.
c 0.30	Pilgrim Street	11.1874	1891	Early N5? (Down?)		Still shown on 1896 1:500 OS Map.
0.36	Manors Station Junction SB	by 3.1874	on opening of Manors Jcn SB; by 9.11.1908		1894: 50 McK&H	Two additional lines Manors to Heaton opened 1.4.1877.
0.36	Manors Junction SB	insp 9.11.1908	13.6.1943 #	N5 Overhead (Up)	43 Style B EP (11.1908)	Semaphores replaced by colour light signals June 1936. Bi-directional working on Up and Down north Mains to and from Newcastle No1 introduced 13 December 1937. Destroyed by fire 13.6.1943.
	Manors (Temporary)	June 1943	13.1.1945			Temporary box after fire - exact locatior unknown.
0.41	Manors SB	13.1.1945	12.04.1959	Variation of LNER 15; below canopy, on platform	IFS Panel	Replaced by Newcastle PSB. Demolished 13 April 1962.
0.57	Argyle Street SB	by 3.1874	2.02.1964	N4 Brick 'lean-to' (Down)	50 McK&H 4" (1904) insp 19 July 1904	New locking 1921. Semaphores replaced by colour light signals 1/2 December 1957. Replaced by Newcastle PSB Extension Stage 1.
1.03	Red Barns later Ouseburn SB (1)	by 1871	1887?	(Down)	signals only in 1871	Mentioned in 1871 accident report. New siding 'Red Barns' inspected May 1873; Block Report mentions '...the signals and points connected and interlocked...'. Mileage as shown in 1871 report.
1.04	Ouseburn (Bridge) SB (2)	1887?	2.02.1964	N1? (Up)	19 Stevens (1887); 10 (?) (1945)	New frame (B) 26.08.1945. Replaced by Newcastle FSB Extension Stage 1.

Mileage (M Chns)	Name	Opened	Closed	Cabin Type and Location	Lever Frame / Panel	Remarks
1.24	Grey's Brick Yard *later* Riverside Junction SB (1)	by 11.1874	by 1885	(Down)		Inspected 15.8.1877. Named 'Grey's Brickyard Junction' before Riverside line opening (1 May 1879).
1.29	Riverside Junction SB (2)	by 1885	2.02.1964	N1 (Up)	32 Stevens (1897); ? (1945)	New frame 9.9.1945. Replaced by Newcastle PSB Extension Stage 1.
1.45	Heaton Station SB (1)	July 1868	1896?			Location unknown.
	Heaton Junction Goods	by 3.1874				
1.47	Heaton Station SB (2)	1896?	2.02.1964	On Platform Between Up and Down Main	Stevens Dwarf frame 14 (1896)	Replaced by Newcastle PSB Extension Scheme. Station roof demolished. Aug 1974. Station closed and demolition commenced, 10 Aug 1980.
1.77	Heaton South SB	pre 1873	5.09.1964	N2 (tall) Brick (Down)	64 (in 1902); 75 (1940)	Included in 1873 Block Report. New 75 lever frame 28.11.1940. Replaced by Heaton PSB.
	Heaton Sidings SB	1872		(Down)		Included in 1873 Block Report - 'just completed'.
2.16	Heaton Carriage Sidings CT	21.3.1977		BR (ER)	IFS Panel (1977)	Under construction, Jan 1976. Introduced to control remodelled layout.
2.34	Heaton (Junction) North SB	1873	1924	(Up)	50 McK&H / Stevens 1892	Included in 1873 Block Report - 'nearly completed'. New frame 3 Oct 1892 McK&H, Stevens locking.
2.35	Heaton Down Yard SB	frame 9.2.1941	10.11.1963	Timber on brick base approximately S4	35	Replaced Heaton North Junction. Reduced to GF status 10.11.1963.
at Heaton East	Heaton PSB	5.09.1964	19.04.1991	BR (NER) Brick	Westinghouse NX (Diagram and Panel Combined)	Heaton North Junction remodelled 6 June 1976. Primary Departure Lines 1 - 6 brought into use September 1975. Remodelled connections to Carriage Sidings and DMU sidings into use 19 October 1980. New panel circa 1980. Replaced by Tyneside IECC.
2.53	Benton Bank SB (1)	by 10.1877	circa 1908	N1? (Up)	34 levers Stevens	New frame 29 May 1904, inspected 18 June.
2.54	Benton Bank SB (2)	January 1908	5.09.1964	N3 Brick (Up)	70 Stevens (1.1908)	New Frame 60 levers No16 pattern 15.6.1942. Closed under Heaton resignalling.
2.64	Coast Road GF	4.10.48		(Down)		Connection to Wills Tobacco Factory; released by Benton Bank.
3.45	Little Benton South SB	25.10.1942	20.10.1963	N1 Brick (Up)	10 (1942)	Replaced 'C' Pit SB. New frame with SB (C Pit superstructure on new base) 25.10.1942.
3.47	'C' Pit SB (1)		circa 1905	(Up) ?		No details prior to 1905. Note: C Pit was a part of Bigges Main Colliery.
3.47	'C' Pit SB (2)	circa 1905	Sept 1942	N1 (Up)	8 Stevens 1905	Superstructure transferred 40 yards south for Little Benton South SB.
3.71	Little Benton North SB	25.10.1942	20.10.1963	LNER - ARP (Down)	25	Installed to provide access from up main to Little Benton reception sidings. Still standing in 1977.
4.24	Benton Quarry SB (1)	pre 1873	1903?	N1 stone (Up) at top of bank		Included in 1873 Block Report: '...a permanent and elevated cabin is erected on the top of the Cutting, east of the lines.'
4.24	Benton Quarry SB (2)	1903?	1.03.1964	N2 Brick (Up)	34 McK&H (1903)	Frame inspected 18.6.1904. (Benton curves opening: west 1 May 1903, east 1 July 1904.) Replaced by Benton PSB.
4.26	Benton PSB	1.03.1964	17.04.1991	BR - NE Region (Down)	Westinghouse NX (Diagram and Panel Combined)	Junction remodelled for Metro 1978 / 1979. Replaced by Tyneside IECC. Base retained as relay room.
4.58	Benton North SB	6.10.1940	1.03.1964	Timber S5 (Up)	15, No.16 (1940)	Installed with new west to north chord as diversion route. Closed under Benton resignalling 1.3.1964
4.78	Forest Hall SB / GB	by 1.4.1889	7.1.1965	N5 Special (Up)	15 + GW Stevens 1896; 11 + GW 1943	Overhead box on footbridge No 44. Reduced to GB 6.10.1940 (released / slotted by Benton North SB). New frame 26.9.1943. Released by Benton PSB from 1.3.1964.

Mileage (M Chns)	Name	Opened	Closed	Cabin Type and Location	Lever Frame / Panel	Remarks	Mechanical / Colour Lights
5.57	Killingworth Sidings SB	by 1.4.1889	25.02.1962	Approximately N1 Timber (Down)	55 Stevens (1882)	Extensive facilities for Gosforth Racecourse. Facing connections from Down Main to NCB Exchange Sidings taken out of use October 1981.	
5.75	Killingworth Station SB (1)	by 3.1874	26 Mar 1899			Proposed in 1873 Block Report. Mileage estimated; new cabin shown as 'on the down side of the line, north of the old Signal Cabin.'	
5.76	Killingworth Station SB (2) / GB	26 Mar 1899, 5pm	29 Jan 78	N2 (tall) Brick (Down)	33 + GW Stevens 1899; 8 (1955)	New frame 18/19 Dec 1955. Gates replaced by barriers 21.7.1974. Reduced to GB (released by Benton 329) 15.1.1978. To CCTV from Benton on closure. Base retained as relay room.	2PL
7.74	Annitsford Colliery Jct *later renamed* Dudley (Station / Colliery) SB		Jan 1980*	N1 Brick (Down) extension at north end	24 Stevens (14.2.1904) 41+GW McK&H No16, 1920	Proposed in 1873 Block Report. New independents 1920 and SB extended at north end (inspected 15 Sept 1920). Passenger Loops taken out of use 15 Dec 1968. * WON states closure on 2.12.1979 but this was delayed. Later reduced to pedestrian crossing only.	4PL
8.45	Dam Dykes GB / SB	GB in 1873; new SB in 1920	9.09.1973	GB (Down); SB: N4 Brick (Up)	GB: 10 Tweedy dwarf and Stevens locking, covered. SB: 21 + GW No16, later 5	Siding connected to Down Main south of LC mentioned as being 16 years old in 1873. New SB (replacing GF at 8m.46c) inspected Sep 1920, opened with new goods loops to/from Dudley. Loops re-inspected and approved for passenger trains, Aug 1929. Reduced to GB 3.6.1962. 5 levers No16 pattern (released by Dudley Colliery). To CCTV from Dudley 9.9.1973; transferred to Benton, then to Tyneside IECC.	4PL
9.07	Cramlington Colliery Junction	pre 1873	by 1926	Brick (Up)	5 Stevens dwarf 1904	Included in 1873 Block Report. Base used as PW hut in 1926.	
9.42	Cramlington Station GF		1966	(Up)		For Up sidings.	
9.63	Cramlington SB (2)	1904?	3.06.1962	N1 Brick (Up)	34 (1904) Stevens	Replaced by GF for Up siding on closure.	2PL
9.70	Cramlington SB (1)	by 3.1874	1904?			Included in 1873 Block Report - open platform frame 'only requires a suitable cabin built over it'. Mileage estimated.	
11.38	Plessey SB / GB	by 3.1874	30.10.1977	N1 Brick (Down)	20 + GW Stevens (1898); unknown (1939); 6 + GW No16 (1961)	Proposed in 1873 Block Report. New frame 7.3.1939 including king lever. New frame 12.11.1961. Reduced to GB (Released by Stannington) 3.6.1962. Gates replaced by barriers 10/11.9.1977. To CCTV from Stannington on closure - building demolished. Reduced to pedestrian crossing Aug 1979.	
11.40	Plessey GF	19.6.1960	17.3.1968	(Up)	2 levers	Mileage estimated. Installed to work facing crossover.	
11.46	Plessey Goods Yard GF	12.11.1961	17.3.1968	(Down)	2 levers	Worked mains crossover and goods yard points.	
11.55	Plessey Station GF		Prog 7 1939	(Down)	Tweedy frame, Stevens locking, 5 levers, uncovered.		
13.73	Stannington GF	17.7.1960	17.2.1974	(Up)	2 levers	Worked facing crossover south of LC; released by Annetts key attached to lever 20 in SB.	
13.75	Netherton (Colliery) *renamed* Stannington	1873	3.03.1991	N1 Brick extended 1953 (Up)	1899: 28 + GW Stevens. 1954: 31 + GW No17	Proposed in 1873 Block Report. Renamed 1 Jan 1892. New independents to/from Clifton inspected 15 Sep 1920. King lever in use by 1928. New frame (B) 28.11.1954. Gates replaced by barriers 12.3.1972. Up and Down Passenger Loops dispensed with 25.6.1967 New NX panel 3 Oct 1977, replaced 1981. To CCTV from Morpeth on closure. Base retained as relay room.	4PL

Mileage (M Chns)	Name	Opened	Closed	Cabin Type and Location	Lever Frame / Panel	Remarks	Mechanical	Colour Lights
	Stannington Crossover GF	Oct 1977			1	Worked mains trailing crossover.		
14.51	Clifton Independent GF	1921			2 Stevens	Mileage estimated; shown in RoL (Slater's Manure Siding) - line diagram shows siding connected to Down Independent.		
14.55	Clifton Crossing GB / SB / GB	SB: 1920 insp. 15 Sept 1920	30.03.1975	N4 Brick (Down)	21 + GW No 16 (1920); later GB: 5 + GW	GF: 2 double quadrant levers uncovered 1897. New SB and independents to/from Stannington inspected 15 Sep 1920. King lever fitted 1941? Reduced to GB 3.6.1962 (released by Stannington). Gates replaced by barriers Aug 1974. To CCTV from Stannington on closure, then from Morpeth.	2PL	
15.62	Stobhill	1889 - 1895	1.12.1918	Timber (Up)	8 Stevens 1891	Adjacent to Stobhill NER reservoir and water pumping station.	2PL	
	Morpeth South SB (1)	pre 1873	9.11.1891	(Down)		Included in 1873 Block Report. Same location as Morpeth South (2)?		
16.42	Morpeth South SB (2) later Wansbeck	9.11.1891	29.09.1963	N1 Brick (Down)	18 (1891); 28 (Stevens) ND	In 1905 28 levers. Renamed Wansbeck 18.10 1936 and signalled branch only.		
c 16.49	Morpeth Station SB (1)	by 3.1874	circa 1907			'About the middle of the down platform' in 1873 Block Report		
16.62	Morpeth SB	21.10.1978		BR (ER) 20 (Up)	NX (1978); NX (1991)	North to East Curve commissioned 12/13.5.1980. Resignalling commissioned and new panel provided (separate diagram and console) 22.2.1991 and 2/3.3.1991. Morpeth controls the line from Stannington.		
16.63	Morpeth Station SB (2)	circa 1907	21.10.1978	N3 Brick (Up)	110 Stevens (1905) + gate frame: McK&H 3+GW; 120 No 17 (1937); 120 No 17 (1961)	New frame (120 McK&H 17, 4"; RoL states 110) 29.11.1937. New frame No17, 120 levers Sep 1961. Semaphores replaced by colour light signals 29.9.1963; (RoL states Relock 1963). Frame shortened to 80 levers (41-60/-/61-120) 9.11.1970. Down Goods Loop upgraded to Passenger line status 2.6.1974. Demolished Oct 1978.	2PL by 1936	
16.79	Morpeth Level Crossing SB	by 10.1877	18.10.1936	(Up)	22 + GW Stevens 1897	Replaced by Temple's Siding GF.	1 PL	
17.26	Morpeth North Jct	12/13 May 1980		---	---	Junction point for new north-east curve.		
17.30	Morpeth North SB	19.05.1875	18.10.1936	N1 Brick? (Up)	15 Stevens 1918	On-Call Barriers (operated from Morpeth) with red/green lights. Converted to CCTV from Morpeth 30.4.1986.		
17.57	Morpeth Moor SB	12.03.1903	1918	(Up)	20 Stevens	Note on diag: 'Closed and dismantled 1918' Colliery apparently abandoned 1917. 'Closed until further notice' 1918 appendix, not shown in 1922 appendix.		
18.59	Pegswood (Colliery) SB	pre 1873	20.2.72	N1 Brick (Up)	12 Stevens (1874); 25 Stevens (1909); 15 No 17 (B) (1960)	Included in 1873 Block Report. New ground levers, for signals at new passenger station, inspected 29 Aug 1903. New frame and extra sidings 9.05.1909. New frame 22.5.1960. King lever provided, Dec 1962.		
c 19.14	Ashington Colliery	pre 1873	1907	(Up)	12 Stevens (c 1865)	Included in 1873 Block Report '25 chains north of Pegswood'.		
19.14	Ashington (Colliery) Junction SB	1907	9.3.1939	Timber (Up)	20 Stevens (1907)	In 1925: Ashington Jct. Renamed Ashington Colliery by 1930 (RoL).	4 PL	

Mileage (M Chns) Name	Opened	Closed	Cabin Type and Location	Lever Frame / Panel	Remarks	
20.18 Longhirst (Colliery / Station) SB / GB	1873	January 1979	N1 base with wooden top and overhangs. (Up)	26 + GW Stevens (1903); 26 + GW No 16 (1944)	Included in 1873 Block Report - cabin is being erected'. New frame 20.8.1944. Platforms demolished March 1957. Gates replaced by barriers 19.10.1975. New facing crossover (immediately north of Ulgham Lane GB) and connection to Up Main from Butterwell single line commissioned October 1977. Reduced to GB (released by Morpeth) 12.11.1978; frame cut back to 23 with modernisation of crossing. To CCTV from Morpeth (GFs for crossover and CCE siding); base converted to relay room.	3PL
Longhirst Crossover GF	12.6.1960	21.3.1971	(Up)	2 lever GF	To control facing crossover south of SB.	
Longhirst Crossover GF(2)	10.1977	11.1978	(Up)	5 lever GF	To control training crossover south of SB	
Longhirst CCE Siding GF	10.1977	11.1978	(Down)	3 lever GF	Connection previously worked from SB.	
Longhirst GSP	11.1978			GSP	GSP installed to replace crossover and CCE GFs.	
20.52 Ulgham Lane Crossing GB		22.9.1991	Brick Hut	4 lever GF	In 1905 two double quadrant levers '(uncovered) on up side, not locked with gates. Note on dwg: Superintendents letter of 5 Jul 1930 to S&T Dept 'when renewals required consideration to be given to locking gates with signals'. Released by Longhirst. Gates replaced by barriers 18.9.1990. To CCTV from Morpeth on closure.	
20.63 Butterwell Jct	15 and 16 Oct 1977		---	---	New connection from Butterwell Opencast controlled by Longhirst SB, then by Morpeth.	
22.25 Ulgham Grange SB / GB			(Down)	25 + GW (1902).	RoL states Stevens 1910 Proposed in 1873 Block Report. 'Dispensed with 27 May 1931'. Reduced to GB status. Barriers replaced gates 16.9.1990. Closed 22.2.1991 (to CCTV from Morpeth).	
23.23 Widdrington Station SB (2)	1910	17/24 Aug 1980	N3/4 Brick (extended) (Up)	34 + GW Stevens (1905?); 36 + GW No 17 (1960)	New frame 2 to 6 May 1960. Gates replaced by barriers, 1972. To CCTV from Chevington 17/24.8.1980; then from Morpeth. Base retained as relay room. King lever fitted, 1929 (padlock).	2PL
23.24 Widdrington Station SB (1)	1874	1910	N1 (Up)		Proposed in 1873 Block Report. North of level crossing.	
23.63 Widdrington GF	29.7.1972		2 lever GF		North end of Up Sdg connected to Up Main (trailing points 279 yds south of Stobswood LC), 29.7.1972. GF replaced by GSP for CCE siding 17.8.1980.	
23.75 Stobswood LC (NCB)		17/24.8.1980		Padlocked	LC closed permanently 17 Aug 1980.	
24.63 Widdrington North SB	6.04.1952 (11.00am)	17/24.8.1980	Timber (Down) S5	20 McK&H 16 (B)	Structure recovered from Stonefall Jct, Starbeck. Fitted with king lever.	
24.77 Widdrington Colliery SB	pre 1873	'Dispensed with 13 May 1931'	N1? (Down) 1931'	12 Stevens (1873)	Included in 1873 Block Report. Levers numbered 1-4 and A-H.	
25.16 Felton Lane Crossing GB		22.2.1991	(Down)	In 1905: two double quadrant levers.	See notes on Ulgham Lane re interlocking. New GF installed, electrically released from Chevington SB, 16.3.1952. To CCTV from Morpeth on closure.	

Mileage (M Chns)	Name	Opened	Closed	Cabin Type and Location	Lever Frame / Panel	Remarks	Stage
25.48	Chevington SB	by 10.1877	24.02.1991	N2 (Stone) (Down)	40 Mck&H + GW (1899), Ext to 43 and relocked 1914; 56 + GW (c1933); 56 + GW No 17 (1964)	Proposed in 1873 Block Report. New frame 56 + GW, circa 1933. New frame (B) 43 Levers + GW, 4 Oct 1942. Amble Branch converted to OES working, 7 Jul 1957. New frame 12 Jan 1964. Frame reduced to 31 levers (1 - 25 removed), Nov 1977. NX Panel installed, Feb 1978. Gates replaced by barriers 1978 (Week 30). Up Goods Loop reclassified Up Passenger Loop 21.7.1979. Down Goods Loop reclassified Down Passenger Loop 21/22.5.1980. To CCTV from Morpeth on closure.	2PL
	Chevington GF		11.10.1970			Facing crossover and GF abolished, 1970.	
26.42	Amble Junction SB (2)	inspected 2.05.1900	21.12.1933	N5 bridge cabin	62 McK&H (1900)	Fitted with king lever for Up Independent. Signals crossed OOU 14.7.1932. Destroyed by fire 20.08.1937. Girders demolished 18.10.1942. New points at Amble Jct 25.10.1942.	
c 26.43	Amble Junction SB (1)	pre 1873	1900	(Down)		Included in 1873 Block Report. Mileage estimated from OS map.	
28.36	Acklington SB (2)	by 1.4.1889	12.01.1964	N2 Brick (Up)	35 McK &H (1902)	Emergency Red Trip Wire Warning signals erected on Up and Down Home signals for protection from runway, 7 Mar 1954. On closure GFs installed for Goods Yard (4 levers) and Crossing (5 levers).	2PL
28.39	Acklington SB (1)	c 1874?	by 1.4.1889	N1 Stone (Up)		Proposed in 1873 Block Report - at platform level to allow view of line through 2 overbridges north of station.	
28.39	Acklington GF	19.6.1960	5.10.1969	(Up)	2 lever GF	GF released by Annetts Key from SB installed to control facing crossover. Mains crossover and Down Siding connected to GF, 10 Jan 1964.	
30.60	Southside Colliery SB	9.12.1919	12.01.1964	Approximately N1 Timber (Up)	20 (1919). 'Standard ND frame' (No.28?)	Gate on colliery line replaced by lifting barrier on closure.	2PL
31.66	Warkworth SB / GB	pre 1873	16-20.12.1967	N2 Brick (Down)	23 Stevens + GW (1897)	Included in 1873 Block Report. Up side, east of line, south of LC. Later on Down side. Reduced to GB, 12 Jan 1964. To AHB on closure. To CCTV from Alnmouth, 11 Dec 1990.	2PL
31.66	Warkworth Facing Crossover GF	12.6.1960	11.2.1968	(Up)	2 lever GF	Controls facing crossover opposite SB; released by Alnmouth 62 from Jan 1964.	
31.69	Warkworth Trailing Crossover GF	17.9.1961	11.2.1968	(Up)	3 lever GF	60yds north of SB. Controls trailing crossover and Up Siding points. Replaced 5.1.1964, siding removed, released by Alnmouth 63.	
31.75	Warkworth Cattle Dock GF	17.9.1961	24.11.1963	(Down)	2 lever GF		
32.63	Shortridge GF			(Up)	3 lever GF	NER Dwarf Lever Frame, uncovered.	
33.30	Lane House Crossing GB		1925	Stone Hut (Up)	2 symp gates plus gate board	Replaced by Shilbottle Colliery Junction SB 7 yd further north.	
33.30	Shilbottle Colliery SB later Shilbottle	Inspected 28 May 1925	12.01.1964	(Up)	24 McK&H 5" (1925)	In 1925, gates opened away from tracks. Abandoned trailing crossover and facing points Down Main to Down Sidings, Exchange & Colliery Sidings, 21 Feb 1978. Colliery closed 1980.	
33.72	Wooden Gate GB / SB	GB closed and new SB open 14.8.1921	As a block post: 12.01.1964	N4 Brick (Down)	GB: 2 quadrant frame levers. SB: 26 + GW McK&H No 16	New Up and Down Independents to Alnmouth. Aug 1921. Conversion to 'on call' barriers completed after closure as block post. Gates replaced by barriers, 21 Jan 1963. 20.4.1986: Closed - to CCTV (+ GSP for Xover). 11.12.1990: Control transferred to Alnmouth.Reduced to pedestrian crossing with red/green lights.	4PL

Mileage (M Chns)	Name	Opened	Closed	Cabin Type and Location	Lever Frame / Panel	Remarks	
34.43	Alnmouth Relief Siding GF		1921?	(Up)	7 Stevens	Dwarf frame; redundant when independents brought into use?	
34.61	Bilton South SB	by 10.1877	circa 1907	(Down)	30	Proposed in 1873 Block Report. Renamed Alnmouth South May 1892.	
34.62	Alnmouth South SB	circa 1907	1.07.1951	N3? (Up)	60 McK&H (at back) 1907	Very unusual on the NERly for a frame to be fitted at the back of the cabin.	2 PL
34.62	Alnmouth Loading Dock GF		16.12.1967				
	Alnmouth Petroleum GF		16.12.1967				
34.65	Alnmouth South GF	circa 1907		(Down)		On platform, works points from No 2 Siding (Down) and Loading Dock (Up) when South SB closed; released from North SB. Mileage estimated.	
c 34.75	Bilton North SB later Alnmouth North (1)	by 10.1877	25.3.1907	(Up)		Proposed in 1873 Block Report, 40 yds north of Up platform. Renamed Alnmouth North May 1892.	
34.76	Alnmouth North SB(2) later Alnmouth	25.03.1907		N3 Brick (Up)	116 Stevens (1907); ? (1919); 95 (1938); IFS panel (1964); NX panels (1976, 1990)	In 1907 fitted with two king levers (in effect release levers) for GF at Alnmouth South. New frame, 10 Oct 1919 ? (not supported by RoL entry). New frame, 10 Oct 1938. Renamed Alnmouth, 1 Jul 1951. Remodelling, 10 Sep 1961. Frame replaced by IFS switch panel with GFs for crossover (3) and Goods Yard (3), remodelled branch layout, 23 Aug 1964. Alnwick Branch signalling abolished, 29 & 30 Nov 1969. Down Passenger Loop modified, 25 & 26 Jun 1977. NX panel fitted 1976 (diagram and panel combined). New NX panel (SSI), 11 to 17 Dec 1990 - diagram and pane separate.	2PL
	Alnmouth GF		22.12.1969			Controls facing crossover.	
35.15	Alnmouth North GF		12.12.1910	(Down)	7 Stevens	Dwarf frame (covered); controls conn turntable sicing to Down Main.	
37.35	Longhoughton SB (2)	18.7.1909	4.10.1964	N4 Brick (Down)	25 Stevens (1909); ? (1960)	New frame 10 Apr 1960. Signalling alterations including fitting of king lever, 10 Sep 1961.	1PL
37.38	Longhoughton SB (1)	1874	18.7.1909	Special lean-to Stone (Up)	12	Proposed in 1873 Block Report: ground cabin placed on Up platform against gable of goods warehouse (confirmed by line diagram and insp report April 1891).	
38.44	Howick Heugh GF	1921	17.07.1960	(Up)	3 Stevens GF covered 1921	Signalled Up Line only. Open as required - connection to Metcalfe's Quarry.	
39.33	Little Mill SB	by 10.1875 (temp cabin on same site in 1873)	16.04.1978	N1 Stone (Down)	In 1874: 14 + GW. 1912: 35 + GW. Stevens. 1944: 41 + GW	Proposed in 1873 Block Report. New frame (B) including king lever, 30 Apr 1944. Down Relief Sdg, Down goods yard and north mains crossover abandoned, Nov 1966. Up and Down Independents spiked out of used pending removal, Jul 1967. Gates replaced by barriers 23 Jul 1967. To CCTV from Alnmouth on closure. Base retained as relay room.	
40.39	Stamford Crossing SB / GB	GB mentioned in 1873 report. SB: 1920	16.04.1978	N4 Brick (Up)	GB: 4 ground levers. 31 + GW No 16, 1920; relocked 1961	In 1873 suggested that the Up Relief Siding, which was out of use, be removed. GB with 2 symp gates and 4 ground levers on Down side. New SB 1920 (insp 11 Jul 1921) and new Up and Down lnds to/from Little Mill. Reduced to GB and facing crossover worked from GF (both released by Little Mill). 10 Sep 1961. Gates replaced by mechanical barriers, Nov 1965. By 1969 reduced to 6 levers + GW (0,1 - 5). To CCTV from Alnmouth on closure. Relay room is former outbuilding and not base of SB.	

Mileage (M Chns)	Name	Opened	Closed	Cabin Type and Location	Lever Frame / Panel	Remarks
42.79	Christon Bank GF	29.5.1960		(Down)	2 lever GF	Facing crossover south of SB connected to GF.
42.80	Christon Bank SB / GB	by 10.1877	8.9.1974	N2 Stone (Down)	24 Stevens + GW (1890); 35 + GW (1912); 26 + GW No 17 (1959)	Frame inspected April 1891. RoL: 34 Levers 1912; Eng Reports: resignalled 1912, SB extended. King lever in use by 1932. New frame (B) 12 Jul 1959. Reduced to GB status, 10 Sep 1961. Gates replaced by barriers, 21 Oct 1973. To CCTV from Chathill on closure, then from Alnmouth.
43.29	Fallodon Siding GF		1902	(Up)		
43.45	Fallodon SB / GB	1902?	27.06.1967	N4 Brick (Down)	14 + GW Stevens (1902) plus two platform levers; 7 + GW (1959)	Two platform levers for private station - function not shown. New frame 14 Jul 1959. Reduced to GB status 12 Mar 1961 (Released by Christon Bank). To AHB 27.6.1967 supervised by Christon Bank, then by Chathill. To CCTV under Alnmouth scheme 11 Dec 1990.
43.65	Brunton Crossing GB			(Up)	2 ground levers	Released by Christon Bank from 12.3.1961.
45.49	Chathill Relief Siding (South or 'C') GF		14.7.1968	(Up)	5 Stevens 1892	NER Dwarf frame (no cover). Reduced to 2 levers.
45.50	Chathill Up Siding GF	8.10.1972	11 Dec 1990 (GSP)		2 lever GF	Controls new Up (CCE) Siding. GF replaced by Ground Switch Panel, 2 Jul 1978. Mileage estimated.
45.71	Chathill Crossover GF (2)	8.10.1972	24.7.1978	(Down)	1 lever GF	Controls trailing crossover. Replaced by 2 lever GF, 8 Oct 1972. Control of facing and trailing crossovers transferred to SB, 24 Jul 1978. Mileage estimated.
45.75	Chathill Crossover GF	29.5.1960	Sep 1968	(Down)	2 lever GF	Controls facing crossover south of SB.
45.78	Chathill Station SB	1873	13.12.1990	N1 Stone (Down) special low window for LC	26 + GW Stevens (1892); 40 + 2GW 1911); 23 + GW WB&S (1942)	Proposed in 1873 Block Report: 'Cabin should be erected on site of existing cabin'. New trailing connection for North Sunderland Rly, July 1898. Eng Reports: resignalled and remodelled Oct 1911, new frame, RoL has 39 levers and two gate wheels. Building extended at north end. New frame 1935? New frame, 1942. Relay room added at rear, 1961? Gates replaced by barriers, 11 Sep 1968. BR NX combined panel/diagram fitted, 1979. To CCTV from Alnmouth on closure. Structure remains in use as a mess room.
46.07	Chathill Station (or 'B') GF			(Up)	8 Saxby & Farmer	Dwarf frame (no cover), at North Sunderland Rly connection.
46.14	Chathill Goods Siding (North or 'A') GF	by 1898	11.7.1954	(Down)	3 (1898); 6 Stevens ('1892'?) by 1911	Dwarf frame (no cover); 'North GF' in 1911.
47.09	Newham Station SB / GB	by 10.1877	11.12.1990	N1 Stone (Down)	20 + GW Stevens (9.1906)	Proposed in 1873 Block Report. King lever installed, 1928-31. Reduced to GB status 2 March 1931: functions taken over by No 1 GF at gates (4 levers) 47m 08c and No 2 GF for Goods Yard (3 levers) 47m 02c. Released by Chathill from 12.3.1961. To CCTV under Alnmouth scheme 11.12.1990.
49.17	Lucker Station SB / GB	1873	20.08.1978	N1 Stone (Down)	24 + GW Stevens (8.1906); 21 + GW (1959)	To be erected on site of present 'Ground Cabin' on Down side in 1873 Block Report. In Oct 1897 single line working to Belford, on up and then on Down Main, for construction of Lucker water troughs. During Second World War a king lever fitted to allow working by gatekeeper on night shift (shortage of signalmen). New frame (B) 1959, king lever. Troughs permanently out of use, 18 Aug 1969. Gates replaced by barriers, 3 Jun 1978. To CCTV from Chathill on closure. Base retained as relay room.
49.31	Lucker GF		prior to Mar 1961	(Down)		Dwarf frame for Down sidings.

Mileage (M Chns)	Name	Opened	Closed	Cabin Type and Location	Lever Frame / Panel	Remarks
50.37	Occupation Crossing No 174	25.9.1977				Miniature red/green lights installed. North end of former Lucker troughs.
51.26	Belford Relief Siding (South) GF	by 1890	28.02.1965	(Up)	3 levers (insp 1890); 5 levers Stevens uncovered 1901	Released by Belford SB 34 switch according to Programme 8A.
51.37	Belford Facing Crossover GF	25.02.1962			2	2 levers installed and tested 27 Feb 1961, rel by Annetts Key from SB. Signalling Programme 8A states 3 levers released by Belford SB switch 35. Mileage estimated.
51.46	Belford SB (1)	by 10.1877	circa 1901	(Down) north of LC	20	Proposed in 1873 Block Report. Mileage estimated.
51.46	Belford SB (2)	circa 1901	25.02.1962	N5 bridge cabin	52 + GW Stevens (1901); 51 + GW No 17 (1943)	New Up and Down Independents to Crag Mill opened 1925, inspected 9 Jun 1925. New frame (B) fitted with king lever, 4 and 5 Jul 1943. Demolished. 4 Nov 1962.
51.46	Belford SB (3)	25.02.1962	08.07.1990	BR NE Region	NX	Electrically-operated gates converted to boom gates, 17 and 18 Sep 1966. To CCTV from Tweedmouth on closure. Base retained as relay room.
51.56	Belford Quarry GF		1970 (Wk 34)		1	Operates points Warehouse Siding to Quarry Siding. Mileage estimated.
51.69	Belford North GF	by 1890	17/18.9.1966		3 levers (insp 1890)	Dwarf frame; later 5 levers Stevens uncovered. In 1962: 3 levers released by Belford SB switch 36.
52.48	Crag Mill SB / GB	by 10.1877	25.9.1977	N2 Brick (Down)	15 Stevens + GW (1897); 25 + GW N.D. 4" (No.28?) (1925); 5 + GW McK&H 16) No 16 (1963)	In 1873: proposal to remove crossover. New frames 1897 and 1925. New Up and Down Independents to Belford opened 1925, inspected 9 Jun 1925. New building 1925 according to insp report but this appears to be wrong. King lever fitted 1939? Reduced to GB, 25 Feb 1962. New frame (5 + GW McK&H 16) 7 Apr 1963. Gates replaced by barriers, 6 Nov 1975. To CCTV from Belford on closure, then from Tweedmouth.
54.68	Occupation Crossing No 179	25.9.1977				Miniature red/green lights installed.
54.79	Smeafield SB / GB	by 10.1877	9.12.1973	N1 Stone (Down)	10 + GW Stevens (1875); 11 + GW No 16 (1957)	Proposed in 1873 Block Report: ground cabin west of the lines close to the gates with its door towards them. May have had king ever in Second World War, see notes for Lucker. New frame (B) (11 + GW, McK&H 16), 26 and 27 Mar 1957. To CCTV from Belford on closure, then from Tweedmouth.
55.31	Fenham Low Moor GB		11.7.1990	(Up)	Hand levers; 1 (1960)	1925: 'Hand levers on post' (of double-armed semaphore). GF released by Smeafield from 10 Apr 1960, then from Belford. To CCTV under Tweedmouth scheme.
58.52	Beal SB	by 10.1877	18.04.1982	Probably N1 Stone; extended and to N2 Stone from 1901 (Down)	20 (in 1891); 30 + GW McK&H (1901); 31 + GW No 17 (1958)	Proposed in 1873 Block Report 'on the site of the existing gate cabin which is too small for block working.' New frame, cabin extended, and new Up Independent from Goswick; inspected April 1901. King lever in use in 1928. New frame 20/21.4.1958. Brick extension at rear added, nd. Up and Down Slow lines Beal - Goswick abandoned 20 and 21 Aug 1966. Up and Down platforms removed 1 Mar 1970. Gates replaced by barriers, 13 Apr 1980. To CCTV from Tweedmouth on closure. Extens on retained as relay room. Down Main connected to new alignment between 57mp and 58mp 26 Feb 1984 - maximum speed increased to 125mph 56mp to Berwick.

Mileage (M Chns)	Name	Opened	Closed	Cabin Type and Location	Lever Frame / Panel	Remarks
58.57	Beal Down Relief Siding GF	? (proposed in 1873)	1918	(Down)	2 levers ? (1891); 5 levers (1901)	Redundant on provision of Down Independent to Goswick. Mileage estimated.
58.68	Beal GF (Beal Siding & Emergency Crossover GSP)	9.1.1972			4 lever GF	Controls new trailing crossover and Down Siding north of SB. Converted to Ground Switch Panel released by Tweedmouth, 18 Apr 1982. New facing crossover installed at 59m30c controlled from GSP, Feb 1983.
60.07	Occupation LC No 193	4.4.1982				Converted to red/green miniature lights.
60.67	Windmill Hill SB	by 10.1877	1901 (Sept?)	N1? (Down)		Proposed in 1873 Block Report: west of lines, south of LC. Renamed Goswick 1 Jan 1898.
60.67	Goswick SB	1901 (Sept?)	28.03.1982	N2 Brick with N4 roof (Up)	26 + GW McK&H (1901); 26 + GW No 17 (1958)	New Down Independent from Beal inspected 20 June 1918. New frame (B) 15 and 16 Jun 1958. Up and Down Slow lines to Beal abandoned, 20 and 21 Aug 1966. Separate Up and Down block bells to Tweedmouth so that Scremerston knows from which direction trains are approaching. Gates replaced by barriers, 10 Dec 1978. By 1979 only levers 1,10,15 left in frame. To CCTV from Tweedmouth on closure. Base retained as relay room.
62.47	Scremerston Lime Works SB	13.11.1874	11.1909	(Down)	5 Stevens (covered)	Proposed in 1873 Block Report. New frame 1907. 'A porter attends when required'. Siding closed Nov 1909.
63.46	Scremerston SB / GB	by 10.1877	15.03.1981	N1 Stone (Down)	20 + GW Stevens (9.1908); 16 + GW (1958)	Proposed in 1873 Block Report. Stevens frame 12 + GW, 1873, 'altered 27 May 1907'. King lever from 1934? New frame (B), 23 Mar 1958. Station platforms removed, 11 Oct 1959. Reduced to GB, 10 Apr 1960. Gates replaced by barriers, 6 Jan 1980. To CCTV from Tweedmouth on closure. As at 2010, relay room is not base of former SB.
64.43	Scremerston Colliery Junction	pre 1873		(Up)		Included in 1873 Block Report, mileage estimated.
64.43	Billingdean Colliery SB	by 1.4.1889	1907?	(Up)		Probably Scremerston Colliery Junction renamed.
64.46	Billingdean GF	1907?		(Down)	5 (1907) Stevens	Covered GF, replaced S3. Controlled branch to Scremerston Colliery.
65.01	Spittal Crossing GB		1987	Timber shed (Up); Portakabin (Up)	2; Key locks only.	Originally double quadrant frame, see notes for Ulgham Lane. In 1873 there was 'a through shunt, which is seldom used'. 2 sympathetic gates (Key Lock).
65.44	Tweedmouth Goods GF		30 Nov 1986 (GSP)		5 McK&H (1902)	Dwarf frame covered. Replaced by GSP, 28 Jun 1981.
	Tweedmouth MPD Siding GF	3.12.1961	4.04.1965	(GSP)	2	
65.58	Tweedmouth South SB	pre 1873	3.12.1961 (12.01 am)	N2 Brick with N4 roof (Up)	56 McK&H (1902); 60 levers ND No 28 (1916)	Included in 1873 Block Report. Certain signals altered as part of Heaton to Burnmouth resignalling from 10.4.1960.
65.73	Tweedmouth North SB	pre 1873	3.12.1961 (12.01am)	N1 Brick (Up)	40 Stevens (1892)	Included in 1873 Block Report. New 60 lever frame, Aug 1884. Enlarged 5 Jan 1893. Eight distant signals were worked from Tweedmouth North!
65.78	Tweedmouth SB	3.12.1961 (12.01am)		BR NE Region (Down)	OCS (Push Button) (1961); NX (1990)	New structure 73 yards north of former North SB. Panel installed, 10 Sep 1961. Worked to Burnmouth SB 10 Dec 1961 to 31 Mar 1968, then to Ayton. TCB to Ayton replaced by Absolute Block, 17 Feb 1978. Revised signalling commissioned (working to Edinburgh PSB) and TCB reintroduced, 25 Feb 1978. New NX Panel (B), 6 to 11 Jul 1990 (diagram & panel separate). CCTV for: Lucker, Belford, Goswick, Scremerston, Crag Mill, Smeafield, Fenham Low Moor, Beal. Key Locks with MWL for Spittal.

Stage 2C

Mileage (M Chns)	Name	Opened	Closed	Cabin Type and Location	Lever Frame / Panel	Remarks
66.73	Berwick Junction SB	pre 1873	13.6.1926	N1 Stone (Down)	34 Stevens 1903	Included in 1873 Block Report: 'a permanent ground cabin west of the lines… rather small but will do for what block working is required'. Replaced by Berwick Station SB.
67.01	Berwick Station SB	13.6.1926	10.12.1961	LNER (NE)	75 probably McK&H No 16	Station layout remodelled, 1974.
67.09	Berwick Central (NBR)		13.6.1926			Replaced by Berwick Station SB.
67.33	Berwick North SB	9.7.1903	11.6.1936	(Up)	36	NBR signal box.
68.01	Marshall Meadows SB	25.5.1921	10.12.1961	(Up)	44 Stevens 5 $\frac{1}{4}$"	NBR signal box.
68.52	Occupation crossing No 203		22.1.1978			Miniature red/green lights installed
69.67	Regional Boundary					59 m 49 ch from Edinburgh. Moved north: LNER NE Area boundary was at 69 m 24 ch from Newcastle.

References and Notes:

AHB : Automatic Half-Barriers.
AWS : Automatic Warning System.
B : Lever frame at the back of the cabin (*i.e.* furthest away from rails).
CCE : Chief Civil Engineer.
CCTV : Closed-Circuit Television.
EP : Electro-Pneumatic.
GB : Gate Box.
GF : Ground Frame.
GSP : Ground Switch Panel.
IECC : Integrated Electronic Control Centre.
Line Diag : NER / LNER line diagrams in NERA Collection.
McK&H : McKenzie & Holland (signalling contractors).
MWL : Miniature Warning Lights.
ND : (North Eastern Railway) Northern Division.
NX : Entrance-Exit.
OCS : One Control Switch.
PL : Powerful lights, generally installed by 1934 except where shown = mechanical colour light signals.
PSB : Power Signal Box.
RoL : Register of Levers, transcript in CJWoolstenholmes Collection.
SB : Signal Box.
spl : special (non-standard) design.

Empty cell : no information available.
? : information unconfirmed.

Appendix 3B

Signalling Installations, Tweedmouth – Kelso

Mileage (M Chns)	Name	Opened	Closed	Cabin Type and Location	Lever Frame / Panel	Remarks
0.40	Tweedmouth West		1904	(Down)		Mileage estimated from OS Map.
2.36	West Ord GF		by 1959	(Down)	4 Stevens	Moved from Down to Up side circa October 1935 and new mileage 2 m 44 ch. Siding disused and signals removed by 1959.
4.06	Velvet Hall	circa 1880	29 Mar 1965	N1 (spl), timber, stone base (Up)	14 (1880); 15 (1929)	New frame 9 March 1929.
6.58	Norham (1)	circa 1880	Jan 1902	N1 (spl), timber, stone base (Down)		Located on Down platform.
6.62	Norham (2)	Jan 1902	29 Mar 1965	N4 top, N2 base, brick (Up)	20 McK&H No 13A 4" 1902	Still standing (museum).
9.47	Twizell	circa 1880	28 Jul 1964	N1 (spl), timber, later N2 brick base (Up)	20 Stevens (1900)	Cabin reconstructed in 1900: 'The previous existing SB (8 levers) has been raised and a new frame (20 levers) provided.'
12.18	Green Lane Crossing		29 Mar 1965		2 ground levers	Slot on Coldstream No 28 Up Advance Starting Signal.
12.18	Coldstream GF		by 29 Mar 1965	(Up)	5 Stevens uncovered (1903)	Released by Coldstream No 13, controlled outlet from goods yard to Up Main.
12.40	Coldstream (2?)	1887	29 Mar 1965	N1 stone (Up)	24 (1887?); 38 Stevens (1903)	Probably second structure at Coldstream; location of first (prior to A&C opening) uncertain.
13.40	Campfield Gravel Pit GF	by 1865	by 1898	(Down)		Mileage estimated from OS Map. Mains trailing crossover and trailing connection to Down Main.
14.21	Learmouth SB		1907	(Up)	18 Stevens + 4 ground levers	
14.25	Learmouth Siding GF	1907	by 29 Mar 1965	Timber shed (Down)	5 Stevens covered	
15.45	Sunilaws (2)	1901	29 Mar 1965	N4 brick (Down)	26 + GW McK&H (1901)	
15.45	Sunilaws (1)	circa 1880	1901	N1 (spl)? (Up)?		Mileage estimated from OS Map.
17.18	Carham Tile Works GF	by 1862	18 Aug 1930	(Up)	4 Stevens (1880)	Also referred to as Shidlaw Tile Works on 1862 OS Map.
17.69	Carham (1)	circa 1880	1903?	N1 (spl) ? (Up)		Mileage estimated from OS Map.
17.69	Carham (2)	1903?	29 Mar 1965	N4 brick (Up)	20 + GW McK&H (1912 & 1940)	New frame 29 Feb 1940.
20.04	Sprouston (2)	1912	29 Mar 1965	N4 brick (Down)	25 McK&H (1912)	King lever releases Crossing GF when cabin switched out; brought into use March 1940.
20.05	Sprouston (1)	circa 1880	1912	N1 (spl)? (Up)		
20.05	Sprouston Crossing GF	1 Mar 1940	by 29 Mar 1965	(Down)	2	Released by Sprouston. Mileage estimated.

Appendix 4
Gradient Diagram

The gradient diagram was produced in 1905 by the NER. The mileage starts at Doncaster, and includes the additional 3 miles permitted by the Newcastle & Berwick Railway Company's Act of Incorporation to be charged for the High Level Bridge. *(NERA Collection)*

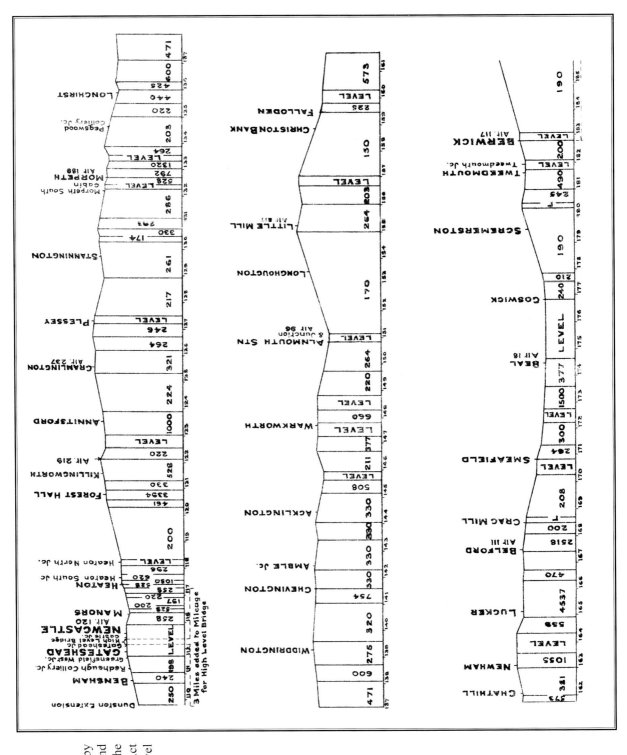

Appendix 5

Diagram of the Line

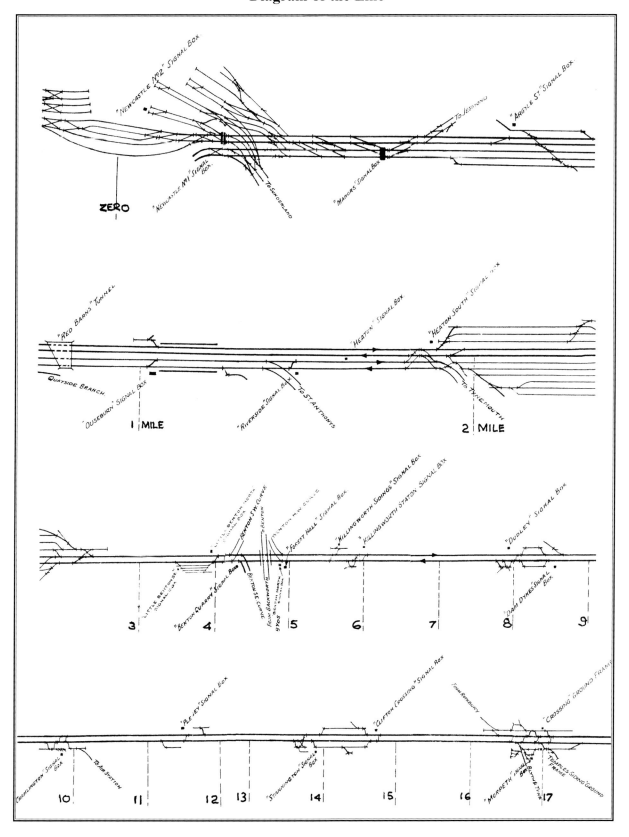

The diagram of the line reproduced on pages 117 to 119 was prepared in 1934 for the Chief Engineer, John Miller, to refer to on his inspections of the line. It shows the main lines and adjacent tracks, but not the station platforms. *(NERA Collection)*

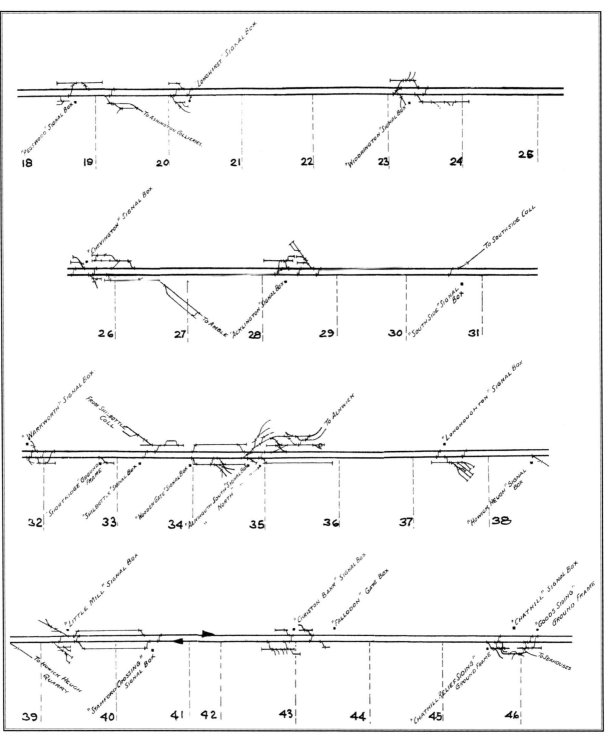

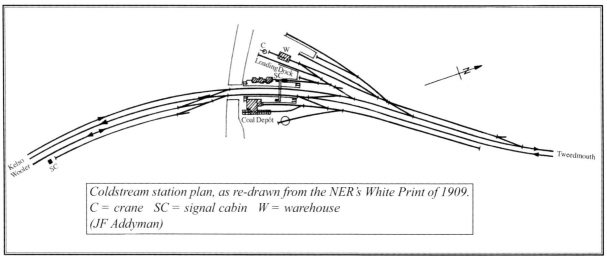

Coldstream station plan, as re-drawn from the NER's White Print of 1909.
C = crane   SC = signal cabin   W = warehouse
(JF Addyman)

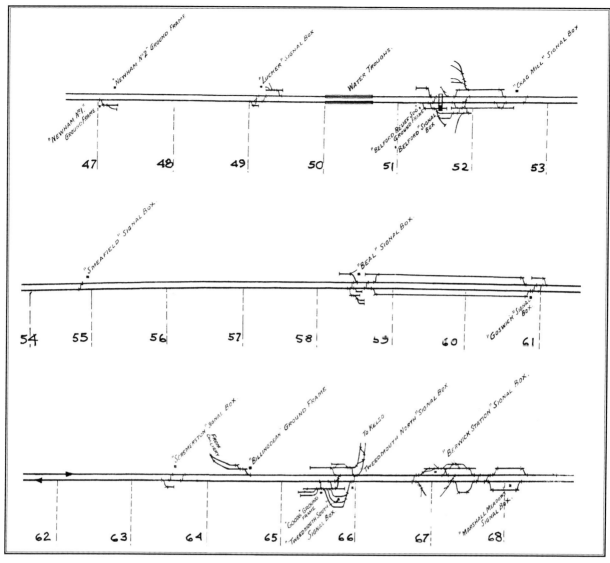

Selected Bibliography

General:

Tomlinson, WW. *The North Eastern Railway : its Rise and Development* (1914 reprinted 1967)

Ahrons, EL. *The British Steam Railway Locomotive 1825 - 1925* (1927 reprinted1987)

Allen, CJ. *The London & North Eastern Railway* (1966)

Baxter, B. *British Locomotive Catalogue 1825 - 1923 : Volume 5A, North Eastern Railway, Hull and Barnsley Railway.* (1986)

Cook, RA, and Hoole K. *North Eastern Railway Historical Maps* (1975 revised 1991)

Fawcett, W. *A History of North Eastern Railway Architecture, Volumes 1 to 3* (2001-2005)

Fleming, JM. *North Eastern Record, Volume 3* (2000)

Foster, CB. (Editor) *North Eastern Record, Volume 1* (1988)

Hoole, K. *North Eastern Locomotive Sheds* (1972)

Hoole, K. *The East Coast Main Line Since 1925* (1977)

Hoole, K. *Railway Stations of the North East* (1985)

Hoole, K. *An Illustrated History of NER Locomotives* (1988)

Hoole, K. *The Illustrated History of East Coast Joint Stock* (1993)

Maclean, AA. *LNER Constituent Signalling* (1983)

MacLean, JS. *The Locomotives of the North Eastern Railway* (1925)

Mullay, AJ. *Rails Across the Border* (1990)

Nock, OS. *Locomotives of the North Eastern Railway* (1954)

Nock, OS. *The British Steam Railway Locomotive 1925 - 1965* (1966)

Railway public and working timetables 1847 - 2010

Rennison, RW. *Civil Engineering Heritage: Northern England* (1996)

Signalling Study Group. *The Signal Box* (1986 reprinted 1998)

Teasdale, JG. (Editor) *Servicing the North Eastern Railway's Locomotives* (2007)

Teasdale, JG. (Editor) *A History of British Railways' North Eastern Region* (2009)

Various contributors, *Locomotives of the LNER : Parts 1 to 11* (1963-1994)

Wells, JA. *Signals to Danger : Railway Accidents at Newcastle upon Tyne and in Northumberland 1851 - 1992* (1992)

Young, AE. *Railways in Northumberland* (2003)

Branch Lines, etc.:

Addyman, JF and Fawcett, W. *The High Level Bridge and Newcastle Central Station* (1999)

Addyman, JF and Mallon, JF. *The Alnwick & Cornhill Railway* (2007)

Rippon, B. *The Amble Branch* (2007)

Rippon, B. *The Alnwick Branch* (2008)

Wells, JA. *The Blyth & Tyne Railway : Parts 1 and 2* (1989 and 1990)

Wright, A. *The North Sunderland Railway* (1967 revised 1987)

Index